A Greater Tomorrow

A Greater Tomorrow

My Journey Beyond the Veil

BY

JULIE ROWE

spring creek
BOOK COMPANY
Provo, Utah

ISBN: 978-0-9960974-0-6
e. 2

Published by:
Spring Creek Book Company
P.O. Box 50355
Provo, Utah 84605-0355

www.springcreekbooks.com

Cover design © Spring Creek Book Company
Cover design by Tammy Daybell

Printed in the United States of America

TABLE OF CONTENTS

ACKNOWLEDGMENTS

First and foremost I would like to thank and acknowledge our very loving Father in Heaven who has given me the blessing and opportunity to share this message. I am so grateful for the knowledge He has given me and am thankful that the time has finally come that I can bear witness of His great Plan of Happiness and of the truths I have been taught.

I would also like to thank my amazing husband, Jeff, who has stood by my side for over eighteen years. He has been my greatest friend and confidant, and has been there through it all. I am eternally grateful for his faith, his strength, his kindness, and great patience on my behalf. We have been through many difficult trials together and there is no way I could be where I am today, had it not been for his care and concern, his love, and his dedication to me and our little family. I am grateful for his strong testimony of our Savior Jesus Christ and for his determination to be obedient to the Lord's commandments. I love him with all of my heart.

I am grateful for my three incredible children, Ethan, Spencer, and Aubrianna. They too, have been stalwart and have been a great strength to me. They have endured much over the past several years, and yet they continue to do their best to follow the Lord and live their lives according to the teachings of the gospel. I could not ask for better children!

I am forever grateful to all of my family and friends who have been there to encourage, support, and uplift me. There are not words to describe what it has meant to me to be able to rely on these loved ones for their examples of courage, faith, kindness, and true goodness.

I would especially like to thank my parents for their listening ears, their support and encouragement, and their guidance. I would like to thank my brothers and sisters and their families for all of their love and support, and for the important roles they have played and continue to play in my life.

I would like to thank my husband's parents, and all of my husband's family, for the many years of love, service, sacrifice, and friendship they have provided. Had it not been for my in-laws, and many other family members, I would not have been able to accomplish what I needed to do to improve my health, take care of my family, and achieve those things the Lord has asked me to do. I am forever grateful.

Additionally I would like to thank my dearest friends, for all of your love and support and for being there for me when I needed you most. There are too many friends to list, but I am confident you know who you are, and I know that the Lord knows of your goodness and the important roles you have played in my life.

Lastly, I would like to thank and acknowledge author and publisher Chad Daybell and his wife Tammy Daybell, owners of Spring Creek Book Company. They have been an incredible support to me while writing this book and it has been an amazing journey. Chad is an inspired writer, teacher, and editor, and I want to publicly thank him for asking me to write this book and for publishing it at this time.

The Lord, in his goodness, made it possible for this message to be written not only in a timely manner, but at exactly the right time. I could not have accomplished this without Chad's faith, encouragement, insight, and direction. He has diligently worked to ensure that the message in this book is accurate, clear, and authentic. I am grateful for his guidance and his willingness to follow the spirit as we have worked together on this project.

INTRODUCTION

The time has come to tell my story. But the question for me still remains, "Where to start?" It is a difficult question, because there are so many little details which have brought me to this point. I struggle to know what to share, how to share it, when to share it, and with whom.

This much I do know, however. I have known for a long time now that the day would come when I could no longer hide from myself, or from the world. I need to tell my story. It is part of the plan, and years ago I agreed to share it—despite my fears and insecurities.

I have known this day was coming for over nine years now, and although I have tried to put it off, and have employed various tactics to delay it, when all is said and done, I know what I know and I cannot deny this knowledge.

It is with the intent to live up to the commitments I made years ago that I am finally writing it down. This is an almost overwhelming burden that has weighed on me for so long. It is difficult to put my feelings into words on paper. In fact, I don't believe there are words adequate in our earthly state to describe what I experienced in the fall of 2004, nor are there words enough to explain what I have since experienced.

I will do the best I can, given my limitations. I just hope and pray I can communicate effectively enough to be able to give the reader a clear vision and understanding of what can only be explained as miraculous manifestations from Heaven.

I pray that those who read these words will find what they are looking for, that they will find comfort in the message, and that they will feel the love our Heavenly Father has for them. He is real. He loves us. He knows us. He wants us to be happy, and He wants us to come home to Him.

First and foremost, mine is a message of love, hope, faith, and healing. While I do not pretend to know all of the reasons I have been given these experiences, I do know some of the purposes behind them, and where appropriate, I will expound and share what I have been taught and told about many of the things I have been shown.

So back to my original question, "Where do I begin?" I have decided to start somewhat in the middle of my story. This would be at the point in time where my life changed forever—when my life took a turn where not only my mind and body were forever altered, but my entire soul was re-awakened and changed. I refer to this time in my life as the beginning of my health journey and the beginning of my calling. In many ways, it was also the beginning of my new life. I have also referred to this time in my life as "The Perfect Storm."

My visit to the Spirit World literally changed my entire being. For as long as I can remember, I have always had a belief and testimony in God the Father and in His Son Jesus Christ. Even as a very young child, I was very sensitive to what I later came to learn was the Spirit of Christ, and the Spirit of the Holy Ghost.

I had many questions about the premortal life, earth life, and what happens to us after we leave mortality. I had concerns regarding where I fit in "The Plan." I had concerns about my family and others. I had great curiosity surrounding lessons and stories I was taught about specific things throughout history, and I had an interest in science.

I often prayed for clarity and understanding to know for myself with absolute surety if the things I had been taught were true. I wanted to know what happened on the Earth, what happened to the dinosaurs, pets, and other living creatures who had died. I wanted to know what had happened to the baby I had miscarried.

I wanted to know that God had a plan for me, and that I was okay. I wanted to heal from the deep aching pain I felt and I wanted to be able to forgive those who had hurt me terribly as a child, as well as others who had betrayed me. I wanted to be able to let go of the burdens I had carried for years.

Most of all, I wanted to be able to love others with the pure love of Christ and to be given the greatest of all of the gifts of God—to have true charity for all of God's children, especially for those who had hurt me. I wanted to be able to be like Him, to truly rely on Him, and to apply the Atonement more in my life. I wanted to not only know that I had been forgiven for the mistakes I had made, but also to know that my perpetrators would somehow be able to find a way back and find the healing and forgiveness they needed.

I felt a very real pain and ache in my heart that felt so heavy it was almost unbearable at times. It literally felt like I had been stabbed in the heart with a dagger. My heart hurt so badly that I had often cried out in agony to God, begging him to take the pain away. At times I wished I could die, thinking about the stories my mother had told me about how I was "her miracle baby."

I wondered what God wanted from me and who I really was. Why had I survived a tumultuous pregnancy and birth, when doctors had initially told my parents I had died during early pregnancy? Why had I come to earth? What was so important in this life that I needed to be born at all? Although I had been born into a loving home with parents who taught me the Gospel of Jesus Christ, for as long as I could remember I had felt a homesickness that I could not explain.

I had struggled to be happy, and I often found myself worrying and wondering, and trying to understand why bad things happen to good people. I had struggled to understand why the Lord allows evil things to happen. Why was there so much suffering on the earth? Why did young children lose mothers and fathers, spouses lose companions, and parents lose children? Why did terrible accidents occur? Why did some come to Earth with diseased and deformed minds and bodies? Why we are born when and where we are born? What had happened to my loved ones I had lost to suicide and other tragic circumstances?

Over time, I had experienced many tender mercies, and I had complete faith in the healing power of the Atonement. I had been given many answers to these questions through impressions and promptings from the Holy Spirit, but I still found myself weighed down with these thoughts. I just didn't know how else to rid myself of the emotional baggage I carried.

I begged the Lord for mercy on many occasions and asked to be healed. Although I had experienced the miraculous healing power of the Atonement in my life many times, I still struggled with self-esteem, self-worth, and with the ability to be able to trust God and truly let go so he could heal my heart completely concerning trials I had experienced in my childhood, teenage and young adult years. I believed I could be healed completely, I just didn't know how.

CHAPTER ONE

———— ❧ ————

The Day I Left My Body

It was September 28, 2004. I was hospitalized for a variety of health issues, with the verdict still out as to what exactly was causing my various symptoms. I had partial paralysis on the left side of my body, migraines, mood swings, fatigue, nausea, vomiting, diarrhea, waking seizures and a few fainting spells. I also suffered from severe memory loss and cognitive impairment.

The labs that came back indicated something was seriously wrong with my liver and other organs. I had elevated liver enzymes so high that doctors didn't believe me when I repeatedly told them I'd never taken any alcohol, drugs or anything else to cause this imbalance. To top this off, I had not slept for several nights straight.

September 28th was also the day my spirit left my body. This was the day that I "went to the other side." I had the very real experience of visiting beyond the veil in the Spirit World. That world is right here on earth—just in another realm of sorts.

This was a day I will never forget; a day which for many years has brought me memories of intense pain, as well as inexplicable joy beyond measure. This was the day I was met by a very kind older gentleman, John. He is one of my distant ancestors.

John told me I was welcomed there and could stay for a little while, but that it was not yet my time to die. He told me that

1

in time, I would need to return to my mortal body. He told me there were some things he needed to talk to me about and that he was going to show me pertaining to my life—past, present, and future. He told me that after I was shown these things, I needed to go back to my life on earth.

John explained that I would be given further light and knowledge about God's plan for me and my family. He told me that I would be shown many things pertaining to me and my family, and some of my future mission in life. He explained that I would be shown some things that would also affect many of God's children here on the earth.

How does one explain what it is like to visit the Spirit World? I think that is a very good question. My first thought in response to that question is, "Seeing is believing." There are truly no earthly words available to be able to describe the feelings of peace, love, calm and warmth I experienced while there. It was all encompassing. It was as though every fiber of my being resonated this love, peace, safety and security.

The closest thing I can even compare it to here on earth is the feelings I get when I am in one of the temples of the Church of Jesus Christ of Latter-day Saints. The next closest feeling would be the love I have oft times felt from my family and loved ones— multiplied thousands of times over and over again.

According to hospital records, I was in the hospital for five days, the first two days of which I "was asleep." It is during these two days, while "asleep," that I was given the blessing and privilege of visiting beyond the veil. It was during this time that I had the opportunity to see and visit with many of my ancestors who have passed on. I was also given the opportunity to meet several other amazing individuals, some of whom have been well-known throughout history.

Let me back up a bit. I feel it is important to give a little more background information into the circumstances I found myself in prior to going to the hospital. I had felt "out of sorts" during the few weeks prior to my hospital stay. My husband Jeff and I were going through a great deal of stress in our lives at the time. I had been experiencing severe migraine headaches, fatigue, memory loss, and a few other symptoms, but due to unemployment, I did not feel we had the money for me to see the doctor.

A little over a week before I went into the hospital, Jeff's grandfather had passed away. Due to our tight finances and having three very young children at home, we determined it was best that I stay in Kansas with the kids while Jeff drove out with his parents to Idaho for his grandpa's funeral.

While he was away, each of our three young children came down one right after another with a flu bug. I was up several nights in a row and around the clock taking care of sick children. At ages 5 years, 3 years, and 8 months old, they were very needy. It was an extremely exhausting experience for me taking care of all three sick children on my own. In addition to trying to care for our children, I also came down with the illness myself.

Normally, I would have called my in-laws or another family member for help, but everyone that lived nearby was out of town for the funeral. All of my family lived out of state. We had not lived in the Kansas City area long, and I did not want to burden anyone else, or possibly get them sick as well.

Having been up multiple times during the night with sick kids, and then at the very tail end of that being so sick myself that I could not keep any food or water down, I was left feeling very weak mentally, emotionally and physically. I ended up with a huge migraine by the afternoon of the third day.

I finally gave in and called a friend. I asked her if she would come over to help me take care of the kids so that I could lie down. She kindly came over and spent the afternoon and early evening tending to the children so I could rest.

Sleep would not come. The migraine was so bad that I was

disoriented, had blurred vision, experienced numbing and tingling in the left side of my face and body, and was so nauseous that I began to throw up several times. I was dehydrated, but could not even keep water down.

As I tossed and turned in the bed in pain, having never felt such physical pain in my life before, I asked my friend if she would please call two elders from our church to come over and give me a blessing. Thankfully, I was given a wonderful blessing of healing and comfort.

I immediately felt my headache subside, my nausea lessened, and I was able to relax enough to rest a bit. I felt much better, but I still felt very out of sorts and I felt a strange sensation, particularly in my forehead in the frontal lobe area. The numbing and tingling sensation continued for awhile, but eventually stopped.

Jeff came home late that night, after having been gone to the funeral all week. He had no idea about what had occurred while he was gone. I did not want to worry him or add to his burdens, so at the time, I did not fully tell him of my ordeal.

He had missed our little family so much, and by the time he got home he was so excited to see us and to play with the kids that I did not want to spoil the fun reunion. I told him that we had all gotten a flu bug, it had been a "rough few days" and that I "was not feeling well," but that was about all I said at that time.

That night I went to bed feeling completely overwhelmed and knowing that I needed medical assistance. It was a long night, to say the least. I tossed and turned and felt as if I was in and out of consciousness.

I dreamed I was in a hospital emergency room and that I was very ill. I dreamed of specific people in the emergency room: my husband, my father in-law, a few of my brothers-in law, my home teacher, my bishop, and one of the counselors in our bishopric. I dreamed of various nurses and doctors who were there talking to me and my husband. They were inquiring and trying to understand and figure out what exactly was going on with my body. I dreamed I was admitted to the hospital. I saw myself in a few different hospital settings getting CT scans, MRIs, lab work done, interviews with nurses and doctors, and so on.

I also saw in my dreams anguish and pain in the faces of Jeff and other loved ones. They were all very concerned about me. I saw my children crying for me, sad that I was not home with them. I saw my mother-in-law in our home caring for my three precious babies and struggling to care for my nursing daughter.

It was heartbreaking. The little bit of sleep I got that night was restless, and when I awoke, I felt a sadness and weight that is hard to describe.

I had an emotional day and I prayed for understanding and clarity to know why I had dreamed what felt like such an awful experience. I was given very real comfort, and feelings of peace came to me that I will forever remember. I had very strong impressions come to my mind. I was essentially told that all would be well and not to worry about what I had seen in my dreams. God was aware of me and my family and He would take care of me and of us.

I tried to explain to Jeff what I was feeling and some of what I had dreamed. He was of course very concerned, so he did his best to care for the children. He sent me to lie down upstairs in our bedroom to try to get some rest the following afternoon. I had never felt so tired in my life.

I went upstairs to lie down and finally get some sleep, and as I felt myself falling asleep, the strangest sensation came over my body. I felt disconnected. The veil became very thin and all around me I could see I was surrounded by the most beautiful women, all wearing white.

I say they were beautiful because although they were of varying shapes and sizes and most were elderly in their years, they absolutely beamed with light which surrounded them and filled my room with a radiance I had never before seen.

A few of them I recognized as relatives who had passed on. They were watching over me with great care. Seeing them there and feeling the disconnection going on in my body between my spirit and my body, I was afraid to go to sleep. I was afraid I would not wake up. I was afraid I was dying. I was very anxious and did not know how to explain to Jeff what I was seeing and feeling.

Every time I dozed off to sleep, I would feel my spirit start to leave my body. It took all of my mental effort and physical strength to keep myself from "floating away." So I would get up out of bed, make my way downstairs to where Jeff was tending to the children, and try to explain to him that I couldn't go to sleep right then. He continued to encourage me to go back upstairs and go to sleep. Every time I attempted to do so, the same thing would happen.

Eventually, I went downstairs and collapsed on the living room floor. Jeff of course became even more concerned. He took my temperature and brought me water to drink. I immediately threw it up. I finally fell asleep there on the floor for some amount of time—I do not know for how long. Once again I started dreaming of the hospital scenes.

That night and the next day my sickness continued, with increased vengeance and additional symptoms. I was in torment. Eventually I had difficulty walking due to a partial paralysis on my left side, being light-headed and fainting a few times. The tingling and numbing sensation in my head and extremities increased and continued. My left side began to tremor, and my right arm stiffened and drew up tight toward my body.

Again I was given a priesthood blessing, this time by my husband. I do not remember much about what he said, although I do remember very specifically that as soon as he started to pray, the tremors in my body immediately stopped. I felt a warmth come over my entire body from the crown of my head to the tips of my toes. It was accompanied by a warm tingling feeling that could best be described as a very real energetic power or influence which completely enveloped me. It felt almost like someone had put a warm blanket over me.

Jeff immediately called his parents and they came right over. He and my father-in-law each took an arm and carried me to the car. My mother-in-law stayed at our home to care for our two boys and baby girl.

We drove to the hospital and I was completely out of sorts. I was confused, disoriented and speaking nonsense. Although things in my body were in complete chaos, and the experience was stressful and intense for my husband and family, I was happy and grateful to finally be going to the hospital to get the help that I so desperately needed.

We went straight to the emergency room. After a time, they found a room for me. They asked me questions, and then asked Jeff and his dad some questions as I was admitted. They tried to get an understanding of the circumstances that had brought us to that point. They did their best to assess the current situation and to discern what was going on with my mind and body.

Time went on, and the room began to fill with people. The scene began to play out just as I had seen it in my dreams. I recognized that this was occurring, and because of this, although I was out of sorts, I felt a peace and calm about the seemingly dire situation. The Lord had tried to prepare me and I recognized that everything was going to be okay.

The veil was still very thin for me. Not only was the room full of doctors and nurses coming and going, the individuals I had seen in my dreams began to arrive one at a time as well. Additionally, there were many from the other side who were there keeping watch and who were intervening in my behalf.

Spirits from the other side were coming and going. It was a very busy hospital room. I felt them. I smelled them. I sensed them. In some cases, I saw them. Some visitors from the other side were there the whole time, while others came and went, only staying briefly. I was continually reassured. My fears and anxieties were calmed by the very real presence of some of my loved ones who have passed on from this mortal existence.

When one speaks of guardian angels, or ministering angels, there is absolute truth in this. Although I did not know or at least don't remember most of those who came and went that day, I do know they were all familiar to me. It was as if I remembered them from another place and time. They were family. They were friends. They loved me and they had been given responsibility over me.

I do specifically remember some of my relatives from both my mother's side and father's side of the family. My gramps (grandfather on my father's side), my grandma Susan (my mother's mother who had passed away shortly after giving birth to my mother), my grandfather on my mother's side, my Aunt Verde and Uncle John, (my mother's aunt and uncle who had taken care of she and her twin sister after Grandma Susan had passed away shortly after childbirth), and the same group of older women who had been in my bedroom the previous days.

I felt loved and I felt very happy, despite the circumstances. I felt bad though, that the mortal friends and family members who had come to help were worried and very concerned about me.

I very clearly remember seeing the look of pain and worry on Jeff's face, and on the faces of those present. The events that transpired in that emergency room are still so clear to me I could easily describe them in great detail in terms of who was there, what was going on, and the level of intensity that was felt by all present. Out of respect and sensitivity for those who were there that day, I will refrain from going into any more detail about this experience. Suffice it to say, it was a very difficult and emotional experience for everyone involved.

I was admitted to the hospital, and they asked me if I would like a wheelchair. I said no, and that I would be fine to walk. Jeff helped me walk down the corridor of the hospital and into the next area. Again came more questioning. We filled out and signed more paperwork, and then due to the circumstances, they gave me medication. One of the medications they gave me was a sleeping pill.

A nurse took me to my hospital room located just outside of the nurse's station. I said my good-byes to Jeff, feeling relieved yet saddened to see the look of complete exhaustion, concern and worry on his face. I sensed his pain and it was all I could do to let him go. I felt awful that I was responsible for causing him or anyone else pain or concern of any kind.

I did not want to be a worry or burden, but I knew that it was all out of my control and that for whatever reason, God had not only allowed this to happen to us, it was actually part of His plan. In His kindness, He had blessed me with a tender mercy and had given me a "heads up."

As I fell asleep, I could still see those from the other side watching over me, and I felt peaceful. Right before I fell asleep, one of the nurses came in to check on me. I clearly remember what she looked like, and I remember she asked me if everything was all right. I answered in the affirmative, and she left the room.

I was left alone in the hospital room, with ministering angels taking care to see that I was comfortable and okay with what was going on around me. As I closed my eyes, all but one older woman (from the other side of the veil) left the room. The last thing I remember, I was singing myself to sleep to the hymn, "The Spirit of God."

I started to dream. In this dream I began to see scenes from my life played out. After some time, I don't know for how long, I awoke briefly. I was disoriented and confused. I didn't completely remember what was going on or why I was in the room. I began to feel the same sensation I had felt previously at my home when I had attempted to sleep. This time, however, I was so relaxed from the medication that I did not fight it.

I felt my spirit rise up out of my body. I found myself standing next to the bed looking down at my motionless form. I looked out the window and into the night sky just as the sun was beginning to rise. I felt my spirit slowly rise toward the ceiling of the hospital room. I rose higher and higher . . .

CHAPTER TWO

———— ⚬ ————

The Lake

Within what seemed to be just a matter of minutes, I found myself in the middle of a beautiful field filled with the most brilliant green grass I have ever seen. Gorgeous flowers surrounded me, and I heard beautiful melodic music. I was surrounded by beauty everywhere I turned.

I was soon met by an older gentleman with blond hair and blue eyes who introduced himself as John. He told me he was one of my ancestors, and that he was there to help me. I immediately recognized him as someone I knew, but I could not tell you exactly who he is or how I came to know him. I do know that he is a ministering angel and one of my many guardian angels.

He is the same man who gave me the "tour" beyond the veil that I am about to share with you, and who also for years had shown me things in my dreams. He continues to be an important person in my life. Since 2004, I have continued to have dreams about present and future circumstances, and he is often the messenger who teaches me during these experiences.

I recognized his voice. I would recognize his face if I saw him again in real life, but for some reason, I do not remember ever being told who he is exactly. Apparently it is not something I am supposed to know right now.

I walked with John across this beautiful field, and we came

upon the most incredibly beautiful lake. It was crystal clear and of a silvery blue color that sparkled in the bright sunlight. We stood together on the shore, and John encouraged me to gaze into the water.

In the lake I could see all manner of fish swimming around. There were varieties I have never before seen on this earth. There were varieties of every kind in several different sizes, shapes and species. The lake was so clear but so deep that it went beyond my vision and I could not see the bottom—as if it went on and on forever.

The water was seemingly alive, and the fish and other organisms that lived in this lake were full of energy and intelligence. I felt as if they were communicating with me. I could sense that they too felt the love and peace that I felt.

It quickly became apparent to me that every living thing, the grass, the flowers, the trees, the animals—all that I saw—were able to communicate with me and with each other telepathically. There was a feeling of true joy and completion emanating from the water and from the intelligences all around me. It was exquisite. It was made known to me that this was Living Water.

John talked to me for a while on the shore. He asked me, "Do you know where we are?"

"I don't know for sure," I responded.

He asked me what I saw when I looked in and at the lake. He talked to me about the Lord's plan for me and for his children, specifically about the fact that I was there in the Spirit World for a brief visit, and that the Lord had a plan for me. It was not yet my time to return to the Spirit World permanently.

He drew my attention to my patriarchal blessing and asked me what I remembered about it and what it said. We discussed that topic for quite a long time. He specifically reminded me about covenants I had made in heaven before being born, as well as ones I had made on earth.

We talked about what had happened to my body and why I was so ill. He told me that although Satan had gone to great lengths to try to hurt and destroy me, that ultimately the choice would be mine. He said the Lord would take even the very wicked acts of others and turn them for my good. I asked him questions about my life, and why Satan and those who follow him would even want anything to do with me.

We had a conversation by the lake for awhile, but I don't know for how long because time in the Spirit World is different than time here on the earth. Eventually we sat down on a large log near the lake, underneath a very large tree.

The tree looked somewhat like a Willow tree, but it was not a Willow tree. I asked John about the tree and specifically asked if it was some kind of Willow tree, since I had never seen a tree like that before. John told me it was a tree not found here on the earth. He added there were many of the Lord's creations found in the Spirit World that were not on the earth, including trees, shrubbery, flowers, animals and other of God's beautiful creations.

During this conversation, John explained some of this and more to me. It was as if my eyes were opened up to various scenes in which I was shown some of these creations. There were flowers that were of the most vibrant and beautiful colors and varieties— far more than what are found on earth and visible to the human eye. There were lakes, rivers and streams, and gorgeous mountain views. I heard the most incredibly beautiful music. It was all very breathtaking.

It was as if every living thing was full of love and peace and such exquisite beauty that I do not have the earthly words to describe how they looked and felt to me. It was all encompassing. I felt as if I was enveloped in this love and I felt the very real healing power that comes from having and being surrounded by the pure love of Christ. I thought many times about how much I loved being in this place, and how although I greatly loved my husband, children and friends and family on earth, I felt such gratitude, joy and peace in this place that I never wanted it to end.

I felt the healing power that came with all of what I was experiencing, and I wanted it to last forever. The thought of leaving and going back to my sick body was more than I could bear.

John sensed my thoughts. We were essentially communicating through thought, so it was as though he was able to read my mind and I was able to understand his. Each time I would have the thought that I did not want to leave, John would redirect my attention to some of our previous conversation and would then continue sharing more with me about God's Plan of Happiness. He was very gentle and kind, but very firm with me regarding the importance and need for me to listen carefully to him and to focus not on what I wanted at the moment, but more importantly, about what I knew was right.

He talked to me about the love Heavenly Father has for me and for each of His children. He reminded me of the pre-existence and I was shown scenes from my premortal life, and some of the roles I played there.

I was shown the War in Heaven, as well as various scenes that have played out on earth throughout the history of mankind. John reminded me about the story of my birth and the difficulty my mother had while pregnant with me.

We talked about this for quite awhile, and I told him that I remembered some of what had happened. I confessed that in my life I had often missed our heavenly home and had questioned why I had even been born.

I asked John why I had been born to the parents I was, to the home and family I had grown up in, and why it was that I had experienced certain trials in my life.

I was very specific about several of them, and he gave me very clear answers on many things, but on some topics he simply said, "In the due time of the Lord you will know all things."

True to my normal personality, I continued to ask more and more questions, and he kindly answered me on most things. When I "pushed too far" and had difficulty understanding completely or did not feel I had been given a sufficient answer to a particular question, he would very firmly but kindly tell me that I had been shown or told what I needed to know for now and that I just needed to relax and learn to trust the Lord. I was impatient. I wanted to know everything right then and there, and I wanted to know for myself, for sure, that I was on the right path.

I expressed my fears and insecurities. I told him of my concern I had about where I stood with God and whether or not I was living up to my foreordained mission. I expressed my concerns about mistakes I had made in my life, and my desires to repent and be clean and pure before my Heavenly Father. He reassured me that in due time I would learn more about my life and my standing before the Lord.

Several times John had to tell me that I didn't need to fear, that the Lord loved me very much and that He wanted only what was best for me. He counseled me to trust him, and to trust the Lord. He explained more about the Plan of Salvation, the great Plan of Happiness for all of God's children. This was the purpose of life on earth. He asked me again to be patient, to slow down, and to listen.

We discussed how Heavenly Father had presented a plan for his children to return to Him. Heavenly Father knew we could not progress unless we came to earth to learn, grow and be tested. We needed to leave our premortal home to be tested and gain experience.

John reviewed The Plan with me. He talked about the Grand Council in Heaven, and how it was decided that we would come to earth to gain bodies. We talked about the importance of the resurrection and how the Savior Jesus Christ had made it possible for all of mankind to be resurrected. He said that through our faith and obedience to the Lord's commandments, we could be saved by the power of the Atonement.

John reminded me that the Lord had provided the earth for us as a place where we could prove ourselves. We were given agency to choose good or evil without the influence of the memory of living with our Heavenly Father. This was a necessary part of the plan, so that we could learn to obey Him because of our faith in Him, not because of memories or knowledge of Him. The Lord promised that He would help us to recognize truth when we heard it again on earth.

John also talked to me more about the purpose of life and of our progression. The Lord wants us to have joy.

Some would be deceived, choose other paths, and lose their way. We would have trials in our lives and would experience hardship, pain, sickness, disappointment, sorrow and death. We would also experience great happiness and joy.

Jesus Christ had been chosen and foreordained to be our Savior. Because our Heavenly Father chose Jesus Christ to be our Savior, Satan had become angry and had rebelled. There was a war in Heaven. Satan and his followers fought against Jesus Christ and His followers. The Savior's followers (all those who have and will come to the earth and inherit mortal bodies), overcame Satan and His followers by "the blood of the Lamb and the word of their testimony" (Revelation 12:11).

John reminded me that agency is an eternal principle, and that when we choose to live according to God's plan for us, our agency is strengthened. Choosing the right increases our power to make additional correct choices. The more we follow the Lord's commandments, the more we improve and gain strength and wisdom. This increases our faith and we begin to find it easier to make right choices. As we obey each of our Father's commandments, we learn and grow in wisdom and knowledge. Our character is strengthened, our faith increases, and we become more like Him.

Even though we have the agency to choose our own actions, we cannot choose the consequences of those actions. The consequences follow, whether they are good or bad, as a natural result of the choices we make (Revelation 22:12; Galatians 6:7).

We were clearly taught and understood that these trials and tribulations would give us necessary experience and would eventually be for our good. If we allowed them to, these difficulties would teach us to be better, stronger, more patient and loving people. We were promised that the Lord would not allow us to be tempted beyond our power and ability to resist (Corinthians 10:13).

I was reminded that when the Plan of Salvation was presented to us in the premortal world, we were so happy that we literally shouted for joy (see Job 38:7). Heavenly Father provided a Savior to pay for our sins and to teach us how to return to live with Him again.

As is taught in the scriptures, Christ was willing to come to the earth and give His life for us. He suffered in the Garden of Gethsemane for our sins. Like our Heavenly Father, He knew it would be necessary for us to come to earth and have agency so that we could choose for ourselves whether we would be obedient to our Heavenly Father's commandments.

Satan, on the other hand, wanted to force us all to do things his way. He did not want us to have agency and to be able to choose for ourselves. His plan was to take our agency away. He sought the honor and glory for himself.

Satan rebelled against God and persuaded many others to follow him. He refused to listen to our Father and to follow God's plan. Refusing to follow God's plan brings sin, and sin brings bondage (John 8:34; 2 Peter 2:19).

At one point in our conversation I found myself wishing I could stay in the Spirit World, but John told me he was going to show me something of great significance. He directed me to follow him, and within a matter of moments a scene opened up before my eyes. I was shown what was currently going on at home with my husband and three children.

To my utter dismay, I saw Jeff kneeling at our bedside sobbing and praying to the Lord. He was in anguish. I could literally feel his pain and it broke my heart. He was crying to the Lord in desperation. He was seeking comfort and understanding and begging the Lord to help him, to help our children and family, and to help me. He was asking for answers and pleading with the Lord.

I later saw Jeff pacing the floor anxiously as he talked on the phone to family members. He was trying to explain the best he could about what was going on with me. I saw his parents in our home, doing their best to support and comfort him, and to help him care for our three young children, especially our 8-month-old baby girl who was still nursing.

Our two sons, ages 5 and 3 at the time, missed me greatly, but they were also having fun with grandma and grandpa there. They could sense however, that dad was not doing very well, that their baby sister was upset, and that things were tense and stressful. Our daughter was crying almost non-stop and seemingly uncontrollably. She was hungry, tired, and angry, and she was upset that I was not there. She missed her mom and she wanted to nurse. She was refusing to eat.

This scene was so heartbreaking that this moment became a turning point for me. I realized how much my husband and children really loved and missed me, and how much they needed me. From that point on, I no longer wished to stay in the Spirit World. I quit fighting it and I began to relax and have a desire to return to earth . . . eventually.

It was agreed upon that I would willingly go back to my body, but only after I was given a "tour" and was able to learn and see more for myself what really happens in the Spirit World.

John and I continued to visit for a little bit more. I was shown various scenes from my life in years past, as well as scenes that would happen in my life in the future. I continued to ask questions, and John would answer them. He was very patient and understanding.

I again expressed my fears about returning to earth to my sick body, knowing that I was in for a rough time and that there would be many trials associated with my health. John comforted me several times, and he reminded me that all things would be for my learning and good.

He told me that there would come a time in my life, in approximately nine earth years, when I would need to write and tell my story. I agreed to do so. He told me that it was part of God's plan for me to write about what I had been taught and shown, and that my message would be one of light and love. He emphasized the need for me to focus on the positive aspects of my experience, and the importance of why I had been given these particular trials and experiences.

It was made clear to me that although I would go through several years of sickness, pain, and great adversity, the Lord would be with me as I sought Him. It was made clear to me that in due time, I would be led to the right people and God would open up the way for this message to come forth and to be shared with more of God's children. It was made very clear to me that Heavenly Father loves all of His children equally and that He wants each of His children to return to Him. I saw I would be part of a greater work in helping God's children come to Christ and to find health and healing.

I was shown there would be specific people who would come into my life at the right times, and that some would be there to teach me, others to help in my healing journey, and that there would be many who would seek healing of their own. A key part of my mission in life going forward into the future would be to serve others and to help them "Open their Hearts."

It was made clear to me that once I returned to my body, I was to work diligently to seek answers and to do my best to find those who could help in my healing. I, in turn, would one day become a "healer" myself, serving those who were seeking answers. This brought great comfort to me and added to my courage to be able to return to my body when the time came. My attitude changed, and I eagerly agreed and looked forward in anticipation.

CHAPTER THREE

——— ✤ ———

The City of Light

After awhile, John told me to follow him. We walked some distance toward a light-colored stone wall. The wall was about four feet tall. I looked at the wall and asked him where he was taking me. He told me that in due time I would learn and understand more, but for now I just needed to trust him and follow him patiently.

I asked John what was beyond the wall. He told me that beyond it was a city. In the distance I could see a little house, which looked like a sort of cottage to me. It was very pretty and peaceful. There were flowers growing in various places around the cottage. I saw a well-kept garden. A dog was running in the distance, around and near the house.

I asked John if he knew who lived there. He said it was a very nice couple who enjoyed living "in the country" on the outskirts of the city. The cottage looked somewhat like something you may see in the countryside in Europe, like a little summer cottage. It was so calm there.

The house looked like such a happy place, and I thought I would not mind living there. This caught me off guard, because generally speaking, I had never desired to live in the country. Up to that point in time I had always preferred to live in "the suburbs."

As I had this thought, John turned to me and said, "You know, you can choose."

I responded, "What do you mean I can choose?"

"You can choose where and how you want to live," he said.

We crossed through an opening in the wall. Instantly I could see there were cities in the distance. I asked what they were and who lived there. I was told that these were Cities of Light.

We walked toward one of the cities. I say walked, because at first we started walking toward them, but then we were almost instantly there at the entrance to one of the Cities of Light. We walked along a brick or cobblestone street. On both sides of the street I saw buildings with people busy at work inside, as if I could see through the walls of the buildings.

Outside many of the buildings were rectangular as well as rounded pots of gorgeous flowers. There were signs out front on some of the buildings. Although they were not written in English, I could read and understand what they said. One of the signs said, "Office of the Recorder." Another sign said, "Office of the President." Some buildings were for "business purposes," and others were residences.

I could see that people were busy at work—that everyone there was busy and assigned jobs to do, such as family history work, temple work, record keeping, missionary work, childcare, and food preparation.

I could see that inside some of the houses and other buildings that records were being written, kept and organized. There was a very real sense of responsibility and assignment associated with what was going on in each room. It was made clear to me that the people I saw were working in earnest because there was a great deal of work to be done. They knew the importance and significance of the work they were performing.

I remember looking in one building and seeing women working diligently at what seemed to be a very rapid or hurried pace. There was a real sense of urgency about them. In one room I could see two women in white dresses who quickly came to the desk of an older gentleman who was carefully writing in a log book of sorts.

The women were not there long. They were there only long enough to report the information and to ensure that the man had correctly written it down. Then in an instant they were gone again. Several people came and went into this room in this same manner, and they seemed to be reporting similar things to the record keeper.

I saw a group of women preparing a variety of foods. They were laughing and visiting joyfully and it was clear they were having a wonderful time together. They were making what appeared to be a simple meal or snack. There was a variety of bread, some fruit, vegetables, crackers and a beverage. Some of the women waved to me as we passed by them.

I could see into some of the residences. I saw families talking and laughing one with another. Children were busy playing with each other, and a few families owned pets.

A bright-eyed little boy with blond hair and blue eyes stopped and looked up at me as he played with his Golden Retriever. He smiled and said hello. His countenance radiated and he looked like an angel to me, although he was wearing regular street clothing.

It was at this moment that I asked John the question, "So, is it true that all dogs go to heaven?"

"No, that is not true," John said. "Some dogs go to heaven. Some animals go to heaven, but there is a place reserved for all of the Lord's creations."

It was made known to me that the Lord also had a special place for those of His children who had left mortality while in their infancy or childhood. This brought me great comfort. At the age of eight I had lost one of my closest friends to a brain tumor. It also helped to explain more about my miscarriage.

To John's comment that "there is a place reserved for all of the Lord's creations," I replied, "Tell me more! I have always wondered about this, especially about things like the dinosaurs. What happened to them, and where are they?"

At this moment, John told me to follow him. We came through the center of town, what seemed to be the main street. We sat on a bench near a beautiful flowing waterfall located in the center square.

We continued to visit. He explained more to me about the earth and the creation, and specifically about the dinosaurs. During this conversation, a scene opened up within my mind and I was shown a beautiful landscape of high rolling hills with mountainous areas. I saw large dinosaurs—all plant-eating varieties—roaming about the land. I also saw large bird-like dinosaurs flying all around. There were lakes, rivers and streams and plenty of luscious vegetation everywhere.

I asked if there were any Tyrannosaurus Rex living there. John replied that another place had been prepared and reserved for them and other meat-eating dinosaurs. I thought this was very interesting. I wanted to inquire further, but John let it be known that this was all I was allowed to know at this time. He hinted that essentially my curiosity had been quenched and I needed to refocus my attention on more important matters.

After some more visiting, John asked if I would like to meet some of the women we had seen earlier. He told me he had some important business he needed to take care of. He was going to have me spend some time with a few of our female ancestors while he took care of some things, but he assured me that he would return soon to continue my "tour."

It seemed almost instantly we were in the room full of the women I had seen earlier, who were busy preparing food. They were still working on their preparations. They kindly introduced themselves and asked me if I would like to sit down. Some welcomed me with a warm embrace. They knew me and although neither John nor I told them my name, they referred to me by name and there was a warmth and familiarity about them. I was a little bit anxious and self-conscious at first, but very quickly found myself feeling comfortable in their loving presence.

We chatted back and forth talking about some of the beautiful things I had seen, and they asked me if I knew why I was there. I replied that John and I had talked for quite some time and that he had explained a great deal to me, but that there was still so much I did not know and understand.

I asked them if they knew why I was there. They nodded in agreement to each other and to me, and smiled. One woman in particular came over and gave me another hug. She was a beautiful brunette with soft, loving brown eyes. I don't remember who she is, but I know she is one of my ancestors. She seemed so happy to see me. She smelled lovely. The fragrance reminded me of my paternal grandma.

A few of the ladies who seemed to be in charge of the gathering asked me if I would like to help. To my surprise, I said yes. This came as a surprise to me, because as Jeff and my children can attest, I am not the world's greatest cook. I do not mind cooking, but by no means do I take much pleasure in doing so. In this setting, however, I was thrilled to be a part of the group and to be included in what they were doing.

I asked them who the food was for. I told them I was a bit confused as to why we were preparing food now that we were in the Spirit World and did not have physical bodies.

They told me that although the food was not required to sustain their bodies on a physical level, the items being prepared had special energetic qualities about them and had been requested by those for whom they were preparing it.

They also had what looked like silver pitchers of clear water that they were preparing. I was told that this was Living Water.

They explained a little bit about Living Water, and the significance it plays not only on the earth, but in the eternities. I will describe more about Living Water in a later chapter.

Shortly thereafter, some of the women left with this food on serving trays and went to deliver what had been prepared. Not long after that, John returned and asked me and the remaining ladies how our visit had gone. I assured him that it had been an enlightening and pleasant experience.

He asked me if I was ready to leave. I responded that although I was enjoying myself immensely, I knew that time was getting short and we needed to proceed with the rest of the journey.

CHAPTER FOUR

The Library

John took me to a large building made of a beautiful material that looked like the highest grade of marble. We approached the building and I was able to touch one of the large exterior pillars. I realized this material wasn't marble, and I asked John what it was. He told me the building was made of materials not found on the earth. It was of a light cream hew with a bit of a rose-colored marbled appearance.

There were several other buildings in and around this same area which were made of the same materials and were of similar architecture. The entrance of the building had extremely tall doors. I do not know for sure how tall the building was, but the front doors appeared to me to be at least twenty feet tall.

Outside on the front of the building words were inscribed in the stone. Although written in the same language I had seen earlier, I was again able to read and understand what the writing said. I took this moment to ask John about the writing I was seeing. It was made known to me that the words I was reading were written in the Adamic Language. This is the language we all spoke in the premortal world and that Adam spoke when he was on the earth. I understood the writing to mean, "Place of Learning," or in modern English terms, "Library."

As we approached the steps, a few men in white robes with

hoods came out of the building and a few more passed by us and entered into the library. A few of the men greeted John, and he briefly introduced me as a "visitor." They seemed to know and understand what this meant, and they smiled warmly at me. Then they were quickly on their way to their next destination.

As we entered the library, I noticed there were people—both men and women—sitting at several large rectangular tables reading and studying. These tables were located toward the front end of the library, mostly in long rows. The people sitting at the desks were dressed in regular street clothing that varied in color, style, and appearance. They were so focused on what they were doing that only a few even looked up from what they were studying as we quietly walked by them.

I asked John what they were reading. He said they were each studying different things pertaining to the creation, the world, the history of the universe, and a variety of subjects. I could see that these were individuals of all ages, but they were all adults. There were other people in the library, standing in the aisles, visiting very quietly, or searching for specific books. Some were standing and reading.

In the city there were people dressed in all manner of clothing. Some were dressed in regular street clothing, other people in white robes (some with sashes around their waist and/or over one of their shoulders), and some who were wearing white robes with white hoods. Others had on white robes or light-colored dresses with pastel-colored cloth covering their head and shoulders and part of their upper back.

I also saw some dressed in military uniforms. I wondered who these men were. John clarified that these men were some of those who had fought in war and who had given their lives for the cause of freedom. We stopped for a moment and talked with a few of them. I learned a little about some of the men, and where they had served. They were eager to express their feelings about the fact that they had served faithfully and had given their lives for the cause of liberty. I thanked them for their service and promised them that I would do my best to live up to the blessings I had been given as a result of their sacrifices.

John took me toward the back of the library. I could see what looked to be glass-enclosed offices where a few men were working. I also saw rows and rows of books, high up to the ceiling.

We walked to the center of the library about three-fourths of the way back and stopped. Here John pointed to two large books stationed on podiums or some kind of platform. He told me to open the book to my right.

I followed his instructions, and when I did so, I read the title "Christopher Columbus." He told me to look and start reading the book, but rather than reading every word, he told me to essentially stare at the page and focus my mind. It seemed as if knowledge was instantly poured out and my mind was filled with information and history. He had me practice this exercise three or four times with different sections of the book on various topics. The knowledge was coming so fast it was as if I was speed-reading multiplied by a thousand.

During this exercise, I learned important historical facts about Christopher Columbus, early explorers, and the Founding Fathers of the United States of America. I learned that much of what had been written on earth about these individuals was false.

I learned that Columbus and the Founding Fathers had in fact been inspired men who had experienced personal revelation, answers to prayers, and in many cases, direct communication from angels and from the Lord. I learned that although not perfect men, they had been foreordained to specific missions in life, as are each of God's children.

Columbus was a man of hope and faith, and he had been prompted by the Lord to find the Promised Land. I learned that Satan and his followers knew Columbus, George Washington,

Benjamin Franklin, Thomas Jefferson, John Adams, all of the Founding Fathers, as well as many other leaders of nations and peoples, from the premortal world. From the beginning, Satan and his minions had set out to destroy them and to prevent them from accomplishing the great work the Father had planned for them.

Columbus was a visionary man. He was a successful explorer, and one of the greatest seamen and navigators of all time. His voyage to America was not due to luck. It was divinely inspired. He was divinely inspired to find the Americas and deliver the light of the gospel of Jesus Christ to the natives he found there. Part of Columbus' earthly mission was to help fulfill the purposes outlined in John 10:16, namely to bring about God's purposes of gathering His children under "one fold and one Shepherd" (Jesus Christ), in finding the "new heaven and the new earth" described in the Bible.

Contrary to popular belief, he was not trying to prove the earth was round. That is a myth. Scholars of that day knew the earth was round. In part, Columbus was trying to prove that it was possible to travel between Europe and the Indies without running out of supplies and provisions. His main purpose however, was to spread Christianity.

Thomas Jefferson was given the task of writing the Declaration of Independence. This was an inspired work. Contrary to what has been taught through revisionist history, Thomas Jefferson was a moral and upright man. He was a kind and gentle man, yet firm in his resolve to fight for our agency.

It was here that I also learned with surety, that Satan and those who had been cast out of heaven with him know me and each child of God who comes to earth in mortality. I was reminded of the lessons I had been taught as a youth, and of the sacred mission given me in the premortal world. It was here that I was shown details of the lives of prophets and apostles from all generations of time, and where I was shown more about the sacred roles of men and women.

I was also shown more about the lives of other well-known historical figures throughout time. I viewed details about the lives and missions of Adam, Noah, Moses, Elijah, Joseph of Egypt, Matthew, Mark, Luke and John, and countless other leaders of Christ's church here upon the earth.

I was shown details from the lives of Martin Luther, John Calvin, and other religious historical figures. More was explained to me about some of the great women who have lived as well. I learned about Mother Eve, Sarah, Rebekah, Rachel and Leah, Deborah, Mary, the mother of Jesus; Emma Smith, Eliza R. Snow, and others from the scriptures and from modern days.

One of the pages I turned to was about Joan of Arc. Images and scenes from her life flooded into my mind and it was as if I were watching live video of the events of her day, the great work she set out to accomplish, and those things which led to her demise. I witnessed her death, as well as the lives and deaths of many other martyrs who had suffered and died for their testimonies of Christ.

I then saw a great panorama of historic events. I clearly remember these because I was shown these scenes in the library, as well as later on my journey—through the "Window of Heaven."

Adam and Eve

Our first parents were tremendous people. They were very kind and loving toward each other, and also to their children. I was happy to see that even after they left the Garden of Eden, they were still regularly in contact with the Lord. The veil between worlds was very thin, and they also received many visits from angels to counsel and guide them.

It was fascinating to watch their family multiply quickly, and it wasn't too many years before there were several hundred people in their community. They were taught how to weave, and they made a variety of robes and dresses, which were usually knee-length or longer. I was surprised to see they were somewhat of a nomadic people, and sometimes the Lord would command certain families to go settle a new area some distance from Adam's home.

Adam held the Holy Priesthood, and the Lord had him organize his family into Church units, just as Jesus did in Jerusalem, and as the LDS Church is organized today. The Plan of Salvation was taught, priesthood power was given, and ordinances were administered. They were truly a fair and delightsome people, filled with the light of Christ.

Unfortunately, the thin veil meant that Satan was able to readily influence many of their children, and that became a major concern for Adam and Eve. They dealt with the same issues we face today. I saw the clothing hemlines creep higher among some of the children and grandchildren to the point of immodesty, and wickedness became prevalent in some families.

A crucial turning point that divided the family came when Cain murdered Abel. This was the first murder on earth, and it affected everyone. There was much sadness and confusion as they wept over the loss of Abel. I thought it was especially touching, though, that after Abel's burial Adam built an altar and offered sacrifice. Even in this terrible moment, Adam taught his children about the power of the Atonement.

Justice was served, however, and Cain was excommunicated from the Church. The Lord placed a mark on his skin to identify him and his future posterity, but this was not the curse that is mentioned in the scriptures. The actual true cursing was that he lost his membership in the Church and thus his priesthood power, as well as the Gift of the Holy Ghost. He became an angry, vengeful man, and he taught his family to hate those who followed Father Adam. Satan encouraged Cain to start a false church and introduce false doctrine, including idol worship.

Cain and his followers soon separated themselves from the main group, and it wasn't long before there were conflicts between the people. I saw, though, that Adam's righteous children were able to exercise their priesthood to defend themselves both physically and spiritually and the division between the righteous and the wicked became very pronounced over the next several generations.

Enoch

Enoch was part of the righteous patriarchal line that descended through Adam's son Seth, and he became a powerful prophet. Wickedness was raging across the land, but Enoch and his family followed the counsel of the Lord and began to build a city where the righteous could gather. I was impressed with their humility, faith, and obedience. The City of Enoch started small, but it eventually grew to include thousands of people.

Through their righteousness, the City of Enoch was granted the privilege of having heavenly assistance as they built their great city. The city's centerpiece was a magnificent temple. The whole city was somehow lit by the power of God. The buildings and streets were immaculate, and I could sense a tangible heavenly energy there.

I also saw how the city was protected from enemies. There was an invisible yet real protective barrier that enveloped the entire city like a bubble. This protective barrier was done according to their faith and obedience and was made possible through the power of the priesthood. There were also legions of angels watching over them.

This stopped both mortal enemies as well as demonic forces from entering the city. Eventually the inhabitants of the city become so righteous that the city was literally taken to heaven.

It was awe-inspiring to see an entire city—buildings, trees, soil, and people—elevate into the air and leave the earth. It will be just as inspiring when the city returns to earth prior to the Second Coming.

The righteous people in this city are a reminder that the Lord blesses us when we obey his commandments, and as the events of the last days transpire, we can receive that same kind of protection through our obedience and faithfulness.

Noah

I was then shown the prophet Noah and his experience in building the Ark before the Great Flood that would cleanse the earth. Many of us have heard the Biblical version several times, but I was not expecting the emotional impact this story would have on me.

Noah was strong yet gentle. He had a large family, but most of them had completely rebelled against God. This wicked majority continually mocked Noah and those who were righteous, as he and his righteous relatives prepared and built the ark. Building the ark took approximately 120 years.

During this time, Noah continually begged and pleaded with the people to repent and live the gospel. He not only did his best to teach the people himself, he sent missionaries out to spread the message of repentance.

Sadly, the message went unheeded. It had not rained for a long time, and Noah's message of a Great Flood sounded ridiculous to the unrighteous and hard-hearted people. They refused to listen and obey the Lord's commandments, and continued to rebel against the prophet's teachings. Eventually, the earth had become so wicked that the Lord told Noah the time had come for the earth to be cleansed.

As the Ark neared completion, it was a great trial of faith for

Noah and his wife as they realized what was soon to come. They prayed earnestly for the Lord to give them more time to bring their posterity back to righteousness, but the Lord told him that they couldn't wait any longer. Although Noah had done all in his power to convince the people of their need to repent and obey the Lord, ultimately he had to come to the sad conclusion that most of his family and those he knew would end up paying the consequences of their wicked choices.

The Ark itself was massive, and truly an engineering marvel. It was flat on top, with an oval-shaped design with rounded edges that was completely sealed. The Lord had guided Noah through the whole process of building separate compartments for the people and animals, and even had an area to plant seeds and grow food. Noah and his family lived on the top level, with animals on lower levels, and the Lord showed Noah how to keep things as sanitary as possible.

I found it interesting that Noah did not go out and capture most of the animals. In most cases, the Lord prompted the animals to go to the Ark. At the proper time, they began to appear. The smaller, calmer animals came first, then larger animals in succession. Finally came the more ferocious ones, such as the lions and bears. Noah was able to use the priesthood to subdue the animals' natural tendencies, including their eating habits. It truly was a case where the power of heaven allowed the lion and the lamb to get along under extraordinary circumstances.

When all of the animals and supplies were loaded on the Ark, Noah, his wife, and their three sons and their wives obediently entered the Ark. They watched as ministering angels closed the doors behind them. The angels then sealed up the doors and waterproofed the Ark. Once inside, Noah and his family were no longer able to open the doors. Since they couldn't build a fire inside the Ark, the Lord provided light through illuminated stones. Similar to what the Jaredites used in their vessels, Noah and his family were given a means by which they could see and light the Ark.

After the angels had sealed the Ark, Noah and his family waited patiently. They could hear people outside jeering at them. This went on for some time, before it started to rain.

Soon the rain began. As the water began to rise, the people outside changed their tune. Masses of people surrounded the Ark, begging to be allowed inside. They even used hatchets and other tools to try to break in. This went on for days, because the Ark was so huge that it didn't even start to float until the water was nearly to the top.

They could hear people walking around on the roof, shouting for Noah to let them in. This was heartbreaking for the whole family, knowing the coming fate of their relatives and others who had refused to repent. All of these efforts to enter the Ark were in vain, though, because the Lord and his angels were protecting it from damage.

At last the Ark began floating. The rain lasted for 40 days, but long after the rain stopped, the earth was still covered with water. This was because the Lord had caused earthquakes and other natural events that brought forth water from the depths of the earth as well, literally immersing all of the land.

It was several months before Noah, directed by the Lord, opened a small panel in the upper wall and released a dove. Initially the dove returned once with nothing, and then a week later returned with an olive branch. That gave Noah and his family hope that their time in the Ark was nearly over, but even after the rain stopped, it still took several days for the water to subside. Even once the water was gone, they had to wait quite a long time before the ground had dried enough to send the animals forth.

I saw that there had been several times during the journey when the animals—and even the people themselves—were getting "stir crazy." Noah was able to use his priesthood to give blessings to his family and to subdue the animals as needed.

Finally the day came to open the Ark. I could see the absolute relief on Noah's face, along with his family members. I found it interesting that Noah didn't just open the cages and let all of the animals free at once. Can you imagine the chaos that would've caused? Instead, the Lord told him the order in which to release them, and then the Lord directed the animals where to migrate. It was fascinating to watch.

Noah and his family actually lived in the Ark for quite a while, even after the waters subsided. They used it as a sort of "home base" since there weren't trees to build homes. They also kept some of the animals for domestic purposes. Eventually they began to multiply and Noah's descendants began to spread across the land.

The Tower of Babel

I saw the Tower of Babel from several angles. It was a massive structure that rose several hundred feet high. It was fairly square with gradual tapering upward. I noticed the people were still working on it, but it appeared to be close to completion. The people had built the tower in an effort to reach heaven, but it also served as a place where false prophets could stand and promote idol worship and other false doctrines.

As the scene unfolded, dark clouds gathered and people began to notice something unusual was happening. Then a great storm arose. A huge lightning bolt struck the tower and destroyed it.

The language of the people became confounded. For some the language change was immediate, almost in mid-sentence.

This event was absolute chaos for most people as they tried to make sense of it. It seemed that the more wicked the people, the more difficult it was for them to communicate.

I was shown a view from high above the tower, and the people began to scatter in confusion across the land. I saw the family of Jared, who were gathered together as a group. Jared and his brother were prophets, and they were made aware of what was coming. They were praying to the Lord to preserve their language, and he granted their desires.

Once again, the knowledge came to me that the Lord is aware of his people on an individual basis and he blesses the righteous. There is great importance of passing on scriptures and righteous teachings to our children.

The Jaredites and the Promised Land

After the experience at the Tower of Babel, I saw the Lord communicate with the brother of Jared. The earth had been divided into various continents, and the Lord instructed and guided the Jaredites to travel and repopulate the new Promised Land. They built specially designed watercraft, which protected them from the raging seas and various dangers they encountered during their travels, which lasted many days upon the seas.

The Jaredites traveled a great distance, and they encountered rough waters and dangerous circumstances, but the Lord protected them and carried their vessels to the new land. As instructed by the Lord, these people brought with them a variety of animals, seeds, clothing, tools and other things to help them begin their new life upon the American continent, where they lived for many centuries.

Abraham and Isaac

I was shown the dramatic day when the prophet Abraham obeyed the Lord and prepared to offer his son Isaac as a sacrifice on Mount Moriah. I was surprised to see that Isaac was actually around 30 years old at this time, rather than being a timid young boy as is often depicted in paintings or stories. Abraham was actually quite old. The contrast between the frail older man and a younger man in his prime made it obvious that Isaac had gone willingly and that at some point he was made fully aware of what was planned. He clearly trusted the Lord and his father. Isaac even assisted in gathering up the wood for the sacrifice, and helped to build the altar. I saw him lay down willingly, in complete faith and trust in Abraham and in God.

As Abraham raised his knife in the air to complete the sacrifice, an angel appeared and intervened, sparing Isaac's life. Both men embraced and wept as they rejoiced in knowing that they did not have to go through with the sacrifice. Isaac not only had no ill feelings toward his father or the Lord, but he expressed his faith and gratitude for the experience.

I saw that the angel stayed with them and explained further what it all meant. They discussed how it was a similitude of the sacrifice that Heavenly Father would make of his Only Begotten Son.

The event emphasized to me the importance of being faithful and obedient to all of the Lord's commands, even when they seem to go contrary to our own desires. It was made clear to me that the Lord would fulfill all of His promises made to Abraham and to His people.

Joseph of Egypt

I saw many scenes involving the prophet Jacob and his twelve sons. There were important lessons to be found throughout their lives, particularly the way Jacob's son Joseph persevered in his challenges through faith and obedience.

Joseph ultimately rose to power in Pharaoh's court, and was able to bless his own family because of it. The overriding message however, that came repeatedly to me concerning Joseph, was the urgency of being prepared for difficult times.

I watched as Joseph was sold into Egypt as a slave. He was young and strong, and his father had taught him to read and write. His education paid off. Rather than being sold as a simple laborer, he was brought into Pharaoh's courts. Potiphar, an officer of Pharaoh and the captain of the guard, bought him from the Ishmaelites.

The Lord protected Joseph and was with him. He was a righteous man and had been taught to work hard. Potiphar noticed Joseph's fine qualities and Joseph found grace in his master's sight, and he served him well. Potiphar trusted Joseph so much that he made him overseer of his whole house and all that he had.

Under Joseph's hand, the Lord blessed Potiphar's house and all that he possessed. Potiphar came to recognize Joseph's talents and abilities, and eventually he gave him command of everything he owned and governed. Joseph rose in strength and power.

I watched as Joseph went about working in Potiphar's house. He was diligent in all things, honest and upright. He was loved and revered by all who knew him. He was a strong, handsome man, and he was not only noticed by the men in Pharaoh's court, but also by many women.

He did not escape the eyes of Potiphar's wife. She grew fond of Joseph and desired him for herself. I witnessed the cunning advances of Potiphar's wife, and her craftiness in trying to seduce Joseph. She attempted to snare him many times, using everything in her power to try tempting Joseph to commit adultery with her. He did all he could to turn away from such temptation, purposefully avoiding her when possible. He made many attempts to distance himself from her, but she continued to pursue him aggressively.

Potiphar's wife was the woman of the house and she was used to getting whatever she wanted. She was spoiled and she was selfish. She had successfully seduced others and she was very crafty. She carefully arranged the circumstances so that she would be left alone with Joseph, unbeknownst to him. She sent her servants away and set a trap. She intended to have him once and for all despite her previous failures.

I witnessed her deceitful behavior as she practically flung herself at Joseph's feet, begging him to participate in wickedness. I saw how Joseph reacted in abhorrence as he rejected her advances and ran from her clutching arms. He did not hesitate to act. He immediately and boldly rejected her advances and fled the scene.

Potiphar's wife was angry and humiliated. In her rage, she attacked him, scratching him in anger. She tore his garment from his body as he fled, and he did not dare go back to retrieve it.

I watched as Potiphar's wife then took her own garments and tore them, making it look as if Joseph had ripped them. She then screamed out to her guards, ordering them to arrest Joseph, accusing him of the unthinkable.

She was completely overcome with rage. Her pride, vanity and selfish lust took over to the point that she cared only for herself. She had no thought or concern for anyone else. She had been rejected and she wanted revenge.

She did not care if she hurt Joseph. She did not care if she hurt her husband or children. Potiphar's wife thought only of what she wanted and could not have, and as a result of her wickedness, she did whatever she felt was necessary to punish Joseph and to cover her tracks. She feared that Joseph or someone else would report her behavior, so she took immediate action to try to control and deceive.

Potiphar's wife knew that the penalty for such a crime would be immediate imprisonment and death. She did everything she could to spin the story for her own benefit. She lied to her husband. She lied to the guards. She lied to anyone and everyone she encountered along the way, doing whatever she felt it took to cover her sins and take revenge.

Her wicked choices brought sadness to many, and her

despicable actions led to Joseph's imprisonment and impending death. Potiphar was initially deceived by his wife. However, in time his wife eventually confessed the truth. He learned that Joseph was innocent of the accused crimes.

Upon learning the truth, Potiphar did not release Joseph from prison. He knew that Joseph was innocent, but he also felt very threatened by Joseph. Rather than having him killed, which would have been Joseph's punishment had he truly been guilty of the crimes he was accused of, Potiphar kept him locked up out of sight.

While in prison, Joseph interpreted the dreams of the chief butler and chief baker. He later was able to interpret Pharaoh's dreams. His dream about ears of corn was actually a message that seven years of plenty would be followed by seven years of famine. Joseph created a grain storage program, which saved the Egyptians when those prophesied years of famine truly did come.

As I watched this scene, I was reminded of the quote given by President Ezra Taft Benson: "The revelation to store food may be as essential to our temporal salvation today as boarding the Ark was to the people in the days of Noah."

When we are faithful, the blessings typically don't come until afterward. Faith precedes the miracle. You won't always see the fruits of faith immediately, but they will surely come.

I was taught about some of the importance of how this story relates to our day. I was shown that just as we have had times of plenty, there will also come a day when we will experience a great famine in the land. The importance of family, of faith and obedience, and of preparing for difficult times ahead was yet again emphasized.

I was given yet another great example of how imperative it is that we do all we can to live worthy of having the Lord's spirit with us, so that we can learn and know for ourselves what it is the Lord would have us do.

It is imperative that we get our houses in order, that we stay away from the temptations of our day, and that we do all in our power to repent and follow the Lord's commandments. Our willingness to listen and obey will determine whether we live or die. Our obedience will save us both spiritually and temporally.

The Passover

Many years later, the prophet Moses was warned by the Lord that a sickness would come into the land due to the wickedness of the Egyptians. The sickness would cause the firstborn child in every Egyptian family to die.

I saw the Destroying Angel pass over the houses of the children of Israel when God smote the firstborn of the Egyptians. It was a horrible scene. It wasn't just babies or small children who died, but older men as well.

The Lord had given them specific counsel on how to protect themselves, and those who did so were spared. The instructions—including marking the door with lamb's blood—were unconventional. Many lacked the faith and obedience required to follow the prophet. Some people essentially said, "That doesn't make logical sense," or "That won't happen to me."

As a result of this disobedience, there were some Israelites who perished, despite the protection the Lord had offered them.

I saw how this relates to us today, because we often fail to do the basics that seem so simple. Sometimes we neglect to listen to the promptings we are given. Often we refuse to follow the prophet and guidelines we have been given because we do not fully understand them, or we don't see the purpose.

Some of us think we are an exception to the rule. We may lack the faith required to obey in all things, instead opting to pick and choose what commandments we will and won't obey.

As a result of our refusal to listen and obey, we put ourselves and others in jeopardy. Our willingness to listen and obey serves as a shield and a protection for us. There will come a day when the Destroying Angel will come again. Those who choose to obey the commandments will be protected. Those who reject the teachings of the prophets will pay dire consequences for their disobedience.

Moses

I saw Moses lead thousands of his people out of slavery in Egypt to the Promised Land. I witnessed some of the plagues and pestilence that occurred because of Pharaoh's refusal to let the Israelite people go. The most dramatic moment, however, was when Moses parted the Red Sea through the power of the priesthood.

That was certainly a mighty miracle, but again one of the main messages that I received was the importance of faith. It was made very clear to me that there was an incredible amount of faith and obedience required for each individual to follow the prophet Moses.

Their ultimate survival required complete faith and obedience to the prophet, as they entered that opening in the sea and moved forward. Some people stepped forward quickly and led the way, while others held back. It was interesting to see some get partway across, then try to turn back as Satan worked on their fears. As the final Israelites were still wavering, the Egyptian army approached.

At that point their fear of the army was enough motivation to begin, but they had delayed too long, and some of them didn't make it. Their desires were not faith-based, they were fear-based.

Angelic forces assisted in protecting the Israelites by creating barriers in front of the armies. I saw that Pharaoh was filled with rage and sought to kill every Israelite, but that his wicked designs were thwarted through the use of priesthood power to hold back the army, and then having the water come crashing down upon them.

I saw Moses obtaining water and food for his people through miraculous means. Manna was provided for the people as they traveled in the wilderness, according to the faith and obedience of the people. I saw the people traveling in the wilderness, encountering various difficulties along their way.

They set up their tents in the wilderness, and I witnessed many of the trials of their faith. I saw the Holy Tabernacle, as spoken of in the scriptures. I witnessed the pillar of smoke by day and the fire by night, guiding them in their journey, according to their faith and diligence in heeding the word of the Lord.

I witnessed the prophet Moses as he went up on the mount to converse with the Lord. I witnessed the events that are written in the scriptures pertaining to these communications and the circumstances surrounding them. Moses did in fact converse with the Lord, and God instructed him just as Moses said.

I watched as Moses descended from the mountain, having been gone many days from his people. I watched as he came down from the mountain, only to find the people participating in great wickedness. I saw the look of pain and horror on his face as he came to the realization that great iniquity abounded. I watched as he destroyed the holy tablets which contained the words of the Lord, and I watched as many of the wicked were destroyed due to their unrighteousness.

I witnessed Moses and others preaching repentance to the people. I saw many of those who had committed great sin, fall upon their knees. They cried out to the Lord, begging for mercy and forgiveness. I saw the countenances of many of the people change as they repented of their sins and were made whole again.

I watched as Moses again went upon the mount seeking

comfort, direction and instruction from the Lord. It was made very clear to me that Moses did converse with the Lord, and as a result we have the Ten Commandments and other key teachings.

Temples Throughout Time

Temples have been a part of God's plan for his children since ancient days. Shortly after the Israelites left Egypt, the Lord commanded them to make a sanctuary. God instructed Moses to teach the people about the importance of having a tabernacle for the Lord. The people donated precious metals, stones and beautiful fabrics for the construction of the tabernacle.

This tabernacle was portable. Although essentially a tent, it was made of the best material the people had at the time. The Lord accepted their offering. The Israelites gathered in the tabernacle and made sacred priesthood covenants essential for salvation (Leviticus 1-7). Once the Israelites had settled in the Promised Land, the Lord commanded them to build a temple.

Many years later, King David gathered materials to build a temple. His son Solomon spent seven and a half years constructing the temple, with the help of thousands of laborers. One of the signs of the Lord's acceptance of the temple was the manifestation of a cloud that filled the sacred chambers.

Not long after Solomon's death, the temple was destroyed. Kings and rulers desecrated the temple, stealing gold and other furnishings, then using them and other sacred items as bargaining tools with other kings. Eventually the temple was burned by the Babylonians when they took the Children of Israel captive.

Decades later the temple was rebuilt and rededicated. Hundreds of years later, Herod I, King of Judea, commanded the people to reconstruct the temple. It was this temple that Jesus Christ himself spent time in as a young man and later during his ministry. He defended its sanctity.

After this last temple was destroyed in 70 A.D. by the Romans, it was never rebuilt.

It was made very clear to me that temples are and always have been an important part of God's plan for his children. I was shown how modern temples serve the same purposes as those in ancient days.

It is in temples that sacred ordinances are performed for both the living and the dead. It is in temples that God's children make covenants with the Lord that are essential to their eternal progression.

Samson and Delilah

I was shown scenes from the life of Samson, including what ultimately led to his demise. It was made very clear to me that although Samson had once been a great man, he fell prey to temptation and disobeyed the Lord's commandments.

His enemies were able to capture him because he disclosed sacred information about the source of his great power to someone he thought he could trust. He had failed to obey his parents and he had failed to keep his covenants with the Lord. Seduced and betrayed by Delilah, the Philistines took him as a prisoner and physically tortured him.

Samson repented for his disobedience and again found favor with the Lord. Through the power of the priesthood, he was able to bring down destruction upon the wicked. Although it ultimately cost him his life, Samson overthrew the Philistines. Samson was a great warrior when he was faithful and obedient. He became weak when he lost the power of God.

It was through the power of God that Samson found, obtained and kept his strength and power. So it is with us. When we are faithful and obedient we are blessed with the Lord's power and protection. When we disobey we have no promise.

David and Goliath

I witnessed scenes from the life of David, beginning with the story of David slaying the giant Philistine Goliath. I watched as he was instructed to take food to the camps of the Israelite soldiers. I saw him approach the camp of his older brothers, and overheard their conversations regarding the battle. Just as it is recorded in the scriptures, David was there when Goliath approached the Israelites and threatened to destroy them.

I heard David inquire about the Philistine, and what would happen to the man who was able to successfully kill Goliath. I watched as David's older brother, Eliab, became angry at him, questioning David's presence there and scolding him for leaving the sheep he was herding.

I listened to David's brave response to his brother and others there, standing up to them in defense of his cause. I watched the scenes unfold that led to David's fight against Goliath, where King Saul attempted to dress him in metal armor that was much too large for his young frame.

I witnessed the courage and faith it took for David to tell King Saul that he would not wear the armor, but would instead go to battle without sword and armor, using only his staff, five smooth stones, and his sling shot. I saw the look of awe on the faces of those present, and I heard the mocking laughs and scoffs of the much larger, experienced soldiers.

It was truly inspiring to see David stand up to the Israelites, as well as Goliath and the other Philistines. He was the embodiment of absolute faith and courage in action. He confidently and boldly went before the enemy, never once doubting that God would not deliver him. He had absolute faith and trust in the Lord, and when called upon to act, he did not hesitate for even a minute. David knew he would be protected, and that God had promised him that He would deliver Goliath into his hands.

David knew that God's power is greater than man's power—no matter how large the man and no matter how powerful the enemy. His example of faith, obedience, and courage serves as a sharp reminder that we can do all things through Christ. It was made known to me that like David, there will come a time in each of our lives where we will have to face our own Goliaths. We will be called upon to put our faith and trust in God, believing that He will deliver us from the enemy before us. Like this stripling warrior, we too must stand for truth and righteousness. We must submit our will to the Father, doing all we can to protect and preserve what the Lord has given us.

David later became a very powerful man. Like Saul, he was guilty of grave crimes, but unlike Saul, David felt great sorrow and contrition for the sins he committed. In spite of these great disasters, David accomplished many great things in his life. He played a key role in uniting the tribes of Israel into one nation. He secured possession of his country. He established a government founded on religious laws and principles. The will of God was the law of Israel.

David's reign, and the government he established, gave the Israelite people an example or type of a better day—a more glorious day when the Messiah would reign personally upon the earth.

Elijah

I saw the prophet Elijah, who displayed great priesthood power throughout his ministry. However, he also faced much persecution. In one scene he was standing on a mountain. He was clearly sad and upset. The people had killed all of the prophets except him. While on the mountain there was an earthquake and fire—then he heard the voice of Jesus Christ, who told him the new prophet would be Elisha.

I later saw Elijah hitting the water of a stream with his coat and dividing the water so he and Elisha could walk through on dry land. Elijah turned over his priesthood keys to Elisha, and then he was taken up in a chariot with fire to heaven. As he departed, he dropped his coat to the ground, and Elisha picked it up, symbolically indicating that the mantle now rested with the new prophet. It strengthened my testimony of prophets, as well as the importance of obeying temple covenants.

Shadrach, Meshach, and Abednego

These three men were sentenced to die by fire in Babylon because they would not pray to a golden idol. They stayed true to their faith and covenants even at the risk of their own lives. I saw the king's servants create a massive fire inside a furnace. The men were thrown into it, but rather than being consumed by the flames, they walked around as if they were fine.

I actually saw a fourth person in the flames that I knew was an angel of God. He helped protect them, and they emerged from the furnace unharmed. It seemed impossible, but it truly happened. This event helped change the heart of the king of Babylon. This helped assure me that the Lord is aware of us individually, along with our persecutions and struggles. There are angels all around us. We usually just can't see them.

Daniel and the Lion's Den

Daniel was a prophet who also fell out of favor in Babylon. I saw him placed in a cave-like pit within the city limits where captives were routinely killed by lions. There were several lions in the pit, but through the power of the priesthood Daniel was able to keep them at bay. He was also assisted by an angel of the Lord.

Daniel stood for truth and was protected as the lions were

subdued and had no desire to attack him. It strengthened my testimony of the ancient prophets and the Lord protecting the righteous.

Lehi's Family Flees Jerusalem

I was shown the prophet Lehi, his wife Sariah, and their family. I saw them preparing to leave Jerusalem, prior to its destruction. Due to the wickedness of the city, God warned Lehi in dreams and visions that the city was going to be destroyed. He warned Lehi that the people were plotting to kill him because he had prophesied concerning their iniquity. He commanded Lehi to warn his family about the impending destruction and to flee the city.

They packed food, water, tents, blankets, clothing, animals and other basic survival items and departed from Jerusalem. The family left all of their gold and silver and other earthly possessions behind, despite the complaints of some of Lehi's children. The group traveled in the wilderness for several days, setting up camp as they went. After they had traveled in the wilderness for some time, the Lord commanded Lehi to send his sons to return to the city of Jerusalem to bring back important records.

These records contained the history of their people, as well as the teachings and commandments of God. In obedience to God's commandments, Lehi's sons returned to Jerusalem. The Lord miraculously empowered Lehi's son Nephi to obtain the records, and he and his brothers safely returned to their family.

Later, Nephi and his brothers returned to Jerusalem and visited the home of their close friend Ishmael. They told him and his family of the impending destruction and of the warnings from the Lord. It was decided that both families would flee into the wilderness for safety, and the children later married.

After traveling in the wilderness for many days, the people

came to a large body of water. The Lord commanded Nephi to build a ship. Some of Nephi's brothers and Ishmael's daughters murmured and complained. They rebelled against Nephi and sought to destroy him. Nephi was freed by the power of faith as God intervened and protected Nephi and those who were righteous.

I was shown that after they successfully built the ship, the Lord told the people to load up their supplies and belongings and cross the large waters into the Promised Land. This required great faith and obedience. I was shown that Nephi kept records containing a history of his people and their journey, as well as records of sacred things. They eventually reached the Promised Land in the Americas.

The 2,000 Stripling Warriors

I was shown many scenes of stories that are recorded in the Book of Mormon, including the story of the 2,000 stripling warriors. As is recorded in scripture, Helaman, a righteous man, led two thousand young sons of the people of Ammon to battle against the Lamanites. These courageous young men fought in defense of their liberties.

They entered into a covenant to fight for the liberty of their people, and to protect their land. They covenanted that they would lay down their lives for the cause of liberty, to protect themselves and their loved ones from bondage.

They were a young and untrained army. They faced a very large, aggressive, and experienced enemy. These young stripling warriors were valiant and courageous, and they had great faith in the Lord. They had been true in all things and had been obedient to the Lord's commandments. They were men of truth, and they had been armed with the priesthood of God.

Due to their faith, obedience, and trust in the Lord, they were able to overcome the enemy. They conquered a wicked, fierce and experienced army, because unlike their opposition, these young stripling warriors were armed with the power of God. He gave them the strength and power they needed, and he protected them from harm.

Although they had never fought before, they did not fear death. They valued the liberty of their fathers more than their own lives. They had been taught by their mothers that if they did not doubt, God would deliver them.

As a result of their faith, the Lord did deliver them, and not a single young man was slain. They fought with such great power and strength that the Lamanites fell down in fear and delivered themselves up as prisoners of war.

John the Baptist

I was shown scenes from the life of John the Baptist, Jesus' cousin who was chosen to prepare the world for the coming of the Lord Jesus Christ. I saw him wandering in the desert, searching for food and water. I saw him preaching to the people, telling them of the Savior of mankind who would soon minister unto them.

I was shown his death and the tragic circumstances surrounding his demise. I was also shown that because he fulfilled his foreordained mission, he has received, and will continue to receive great blessings from our Father.

The Birth of Jesus Christ

I was then shown the life and ministry of our Savior Jesus Christ, and all of the wonderful events that surrounded it.

Jesus was in fact born to the Virgin Mary, and is God's own son. He is the Savior of the world. I was shown that the angel Gabriel came to Mary, and told her of her sacred mission. He spoke with her about the divine role she played, as well as the divine role her future son would play, as the Savior of the world. She was told that she had been prepared for this foreordained mission and that because of her righteousness she would be greatly blessed.

The angel Gabriel spoke to her about her cousin Elizabeth, and of the divine role she played as the future mother of John the Baptist, who would help to prepare the way of the Lord. He also instructed her that she was to go to her cousin, and tell her that the angel had come to her and had spoken to her at length concerning things to come.

The angel said that Elizabeth would be expecting her, because she too had been given divine instruction and had been told that Mary would bare the Christ child.

The angel Gabriel comforted Mary and told her not to worry about what her future husband, Joseph, would think or do, because the Lord would make it very clear to Joseph that Mary had been true to him, and he would know through the power of God that Mary was in fact foreordained to be the earthly mother of the coming Messiah.

I saw that as the time drew near for both John the Baptist and Jesus to be born, Mary went to stay with Elizabeth. The two women were very close and they relied on each other a great deal for strength, encouragement, and comfort. This was a great blessing to them.

The birth itself took place in what looked like a small cave-like structure, but it had been transformed into a stable. Joseph cleaned out the area the best he could, but there was no mistaking that the birthplace of the Lord was in a lowly stable. The humble circumstances provided privacy to Mary and Joseph. The animals there were quiet and subdued as the Savior of the World was born. Angels kept watch and stood as sentinels, protecting the young family prior to, during and after the birth of Jesus.

I saw the shepherds in the fields, keeping watch over their

sheep. I was shown these scenes from a few different vantage points. Initially, I was given an aerial view and witnessed the shepherds in the fields tending their flocks at night. I was given a close-up view of the night sky and the star spoken of in the scriptures. Then it was as if I was standing among the shepherds. I listened as they pointed upward and discussed the unique new star that had appeared in the sky. We were far from any city, and the star shone brightly in the darkness.

These shepherds were righteous men, and they were aware of the prophecies concerning a future Messiah. They were discussing whether this star fulfilled one of the signs.

Then I saw their surprise as an angel of the Lord appeared. He told them of the birth of the Savior Jesus Christ, and he instructed them that they were to follow the star, which would lead them to the babe lying in a manger.

I saw a multitude of angels gathered around the shepherds as they listened to this angel and heard the news of the birth of the Christ child. They wept with joy and gratitude. They knelt in prayer, thanking Father in Heaven for sending His son, and for answering their fervent prayers.

I also witnessed the shepherds traveling a great distance in the wilderness to reach Bethlehem. Upon arrival, they entered the city and asked several innkeepers and others they saw if anyone could direct them to the birthplace. They did not receive much help, but were directed by the Spirit as to which direction to go and where to find the Lord.

In time, they found the Christ child lying in a manger, with Joseph and Mary at His side, just as the angel had said they would. It was a very humble scene, and there was great joy.

I also witnessed many other people coming to visit Mary and Joseph and the Christ child, especially during the first few years of His life. I witnessed the Wise Men as they traveled great distances to find the Messiah. These men were prophets and prominent scholars from other countries, but I saw they were humble men who dressed simply. I saw them during their travels as they set up their tents in the wilderness. Their journey took them quite a long time—at least several months or more.

I saw as they finally reached Jerusalem and approached King Herod. I witnessed some of the conversations that took place between some of them and this wicked king. I saw angels warning the men of King Herod's wicked intentions, and to not return to the king to report on the birth and location of the Christ child. They were guided by these angels to Nazareth, where Mary and Joseph and the young Jesus lived.

At the time of their arrival, the Christ child was a young toddler. As is told in the scriptures, I witnessed these men bearing gifts and rejoicing over the Lord.

I then saw them leave the city and travel to faraway places, teaching and preaching about the birth of the Savior to anyone and everyone that would listen. I saw them spread the message of the gospel of Jesus Christ and tell those they were teaching about the Plan of Salvation and about the coming Messiah.

Jesus as a Child

I was briefly shown a few scenes of Christ as a young child, in infancy leading up to about the age of three. I saw that just like any child, he had to learn to crawl, then walk, and talk. I saw his mother Mary holding him and teaching him.

Jesus had a calm temperament, and was obedient and respectful to his parents. He was taught the traditions of the Jewish people, and as the years passed, Mary and Joseph gradually taught Him who he was.

I was also shown scenes of Jesus at the age of twelve, when in the temple instructing others. Unbeknownst to Mary and Joseph, Jesus had not joined their caravan, and had instead stayed behind in the temple. Upon learning of Jesus' absence, Mary and Joseph quickly returned to the city and searched somewhat frantically for their son. They were greatly relieved to find him in the temple, safe from danger.

When his parents essentially asked Him what He was doing and why He had not come with them at the time of departure, Jesus very simply and straightforwardly answered that He was "about His Father's business." Even at this young age, Jesus had been taught by his earthly parents, as well as by Father in Heaven, of His divine role.

Jesus had many brothers and sisters, and this large family helped shape and mold his character. Joseph was a wonderful example and role model for Jesus. I saw Jesus working with Joseph as an apprentice carpenter, and Joseph used these opportunities to discuss gospel principles with Jesus and help prepare him for his future mission.

Christ's Baptism by John the Baptist

The years passed, and the time came for Jesus to begin his ministry. I witnessed John the Baptist baptizing Jesus in the River Jordan. It felt as if I was standing on the bank of the river, along with about a dozen other people. It was a humble gathering, but I felt the immense power of the baptism and the influence it had on those who were there witnessing the event, both the living and the dead.

It was made very clear to me that although Christ was perfect, He too, as a mortal man, needed to receive the ordinance of baptism by immersion. It was important for him to teach all of God's children that everyone must be baptized by immersion, by the proper authority, in order to enter into God's presence and gain eternal life.

Christ Performing Priesthood Miracles

I witnessed Christ perform countless acts of healing. As is told in the scriptures, Christ healed the sick, the deaf, the blind, and the crippled. I watched as He raised men, women, and children from the dead, and as he cast out devils. I was shown scenes from the life of his close friend Lazarus, and witnessed his death and burial.

I witnessed Mary and Martha and others as they pleaded with the Lord on behalf of their loved one, and as they sent for Jesus to come to administer to Lazarus. I saw the sadness, despair, and confusion in their faces as they tried to make sense and understand why Jesus had not yet come, and why it was that the Lord had allowed Lazarus to die, knowing that Christ had the power to heal him as they had seen Jesus do on countless occasions for so many others, including complete strangers. I saw that Jesus purposefully waited four days before He came and administered to Lazarus and called him forth from the dead, commanding him to rise and walk.

It was made known to me that in part, the reason He delayed His coming was so that He could in fact perform this great miracle. Christ knew that the Jewish people believed that the soul lingered around the body for three days, and that the people did not believe a soul went to heaven until after the third day.

It was critical that Christ wait until the fourth day to heal Lazarus, so that the people would see the miracle for what it truly was, and so that there would be "no mistaking" that Christ had in fact raised this man from the dead. It was also made very clear to me that it was due to the prayers, faith and obedience of the people, that this miracle was performed.

It was a great trial of their faith, and as with all things, faith precedes the miracle. It is after we have done all that we can do, that the Lord intervenes and answers our prayers. Faith is an action word. It requires us to act first, believing that we can obtain the blessing, and then if it is the will of the Lord, we receive that which we have desired.

The Last Supper

I witnessed Christ washing the Apostles' feet and administering the Last Supper as they met in an upper room. They gathered around a low table and sat on the floor, some of them leaning against a wall as they listened to Jesus share gospel truths with them.

The importance of partaking of the sacrament for the remission of sins was made very clear to me. I came to a greater understanding of the significance of the Last Supper, and also of the act of the washing of feet. I was shown how this relates to modern prophets and apostles and the sacred acts of service they perform. This was a very sacred experience.

I was left with a very strong testimony that the Church of Jesus Christ of Latter-day Saints is the true church, with real, living prophets and apostles. It is the same gospel that Christ taught while He was on the earth administering to His apostles and the people in His day.

It is also the same church that Christ established on the earth in the days of Adam, Noah, Abraham, and the many other prophets and apostles in previous dispensations.

The Final Hours

I witnessed the events in the Garden of Gethsemane. There were concourses of angels in the Garden, bearing Him up, as Christ took upon Him the sins of the world and suffered for all of mankind. I saw Christ's suffering on the cross, including all of the things that are testified of in the scriptures by ancient and modern prophets.

When His mission was complete, Jesus' spirit left His body. He had given His life for us. I was shown what happened in Jerusalem, in the Americas, on the islands of the sea, and other places around the world at this time. There was great destruction throughout the world as the earth itself mourned the Savior's death.

It was made very clear to me that every person who comes to earth depends on Jesus Christ to fulfill the promise He made in heaven to be our Savior. I know that without Him, the Plan of Salvation would have failed and we would have been left to perish. I know that His mission was necessary, just as all of the prophets from Adam to Christ testified that He would come, and just as all of the prophets since Christ have testified that He did come.

It was shown that the Fall of Adam brought two kinds of death into the world—physical death and spiritual death. Physical death is when our bodies are separated from our spirits. Spiritual death is when we have separation from God. It is because of Jesus Christ's Atonement that these two kinds of death have been overcome. Had it not been for this Atonement, our bodies and our spirits would have been separated forever, and we could not have lived with our Heavenly Father again.

We have not only a very wise Heavenly Father, but a very loving one. He prepared a perfectly wonderful, merciful plan to save us from death—both spiritual and physical. Jesus Christ, our eldest brother, loves us so much that he suffered the greatest spiritual and physical agony ever suffered on the earth.

It is incomprehensible what he suffered and endured. I am eternally grateful for our Savior Jesus Christ, and for our loving Father in Heaven, who designed a plan and a way for us to return home to live with them again someday. Were it not for Christ's sake, we would have all been forsaken. Because of His love for us, and His great sacrifice, we can be made whole. We can repent.

We can forsake our sins and become new again. We can become perfected. He completes us. He is our advocate with the Father. He has, does, and will continue to do all in His power to help us on our life's journey and in the eternities, to be able to fulfill God's eternal purpose, which is to bring to pass the eternal life and immortality of all men.

As I mentioned earlier, upon Christ's death I witnessed the whole earth in great upheaval and distress. Tempests, earthquakes, fires, whirlwinds, and physical upheavals occurred throughout every land. Darkness covered the earth for three days. Hundreds of cities and millions of people were destroyed.

I watched as the people on the American continent observed the signs and wonders prior to the crucifixion. I saw and heard them cry out in fear as the earth darkened and storms began to rage.

Buildings fell, trees came crashing down, and the earth opened up and swallowed entire civilizations. There was not a single glimpse of light upon the land. Candles would not light. Fires would not burn. It was so dark that people could not even see their own hands in front of their faces.

Mothers and fathers called out for their children. Children cried out in the dark for their parents. Families and friends were separated, and the world was in complete chaos. Many who survived the great devastations rejoiced that they were alive. Others cursed God and died. Several who had not previously believed in Christ repented of their ways and knelt in humble prayer, seeking forgiveness.

When the light did come again, the people rejoiced exceedingly. They mourned the loss of their loved ones greatly, but they were a humbled people. Most were familiar with the doctrines of Christ. They believed that He had died, but they also believed that He would be resurrected. Many had been taught to look for these signs, and this gave them great hope and purpose.

Jesus in the Spirit World

I witnessed the burial of our Savior. I watched as his mother wept for him, crying out in pain and desperation for comfort from her grief. I watched as those who loved Him, took His body from off of the cross, and prepared it for burial. I watched as they cried in agony and pain and as they grieved for their loss.

I witnessed their sorrow and felt some of the weight of that moment. I watched as they anointed His lifeless body with oils and perfumes, and then placed him gently in the tomb that was given Him by one who loved him dearly. I watched as Jesus left his mortal body and went to visit the righteous spirits in the Spirit World.

I saw that He taught the prophets and other leaders there. He organized them into a great missionary force. I witnessed and felt of the great joy these spirits felt as Christ entered the Spirit World and they greeted Him with loving arms. I saw Him administer to them and teach them. He spoke to multitudes of righteous spirits before He departed and returned to His earthly body in the tomb.

The Resurrection

I was shown that on the third day after His crucifixion, Christ took up his body again and was resurrected. He was the first person to be resurrected.

I witnessed as the attending angels approached the men who had been charged with keeping watch over Christ's tomb. I saw the fear and confusion in their faces as the angels took charge of the tomb, and the men fled for fear of their lives. I witnessed the angels roll away the stone to the sepulcher.

I watched as Christ rose from the dead, gently folded his white burial garments, and left the tomb.

I was shown that when his friends went to see Him, these same angels were guarding the Tomb where Christ had been buried. They said to those who sought Him, "He is not here; for he is risen, as he said" (Matthew 28:6). Christ's spirit had reentered His body, and would never be separated again.

I witnessed Mary Magdalene and other women who loved Jesus weeping and wailing as they cried in agony inside and in front of the opened tomb, because they believed their Lord's body had been stolen. I saw the perplexity in their faces and the looks of confusion over the matter. I witnessed as the angels approached the women to tell them what had become of Christ.

The women bowed their heads in fear, having no understanding as to what they were experiencing. I heard the angels speak to them, telling them that Christ had risen, and trying to explain that He was no longer there because He had been resurrected. The angels reminded the women of the teachings of Christ, and spoke to them concerning the crucifixion.

I watched as Mary Magdalene was weeping outside of the tomb, and as Christ approached her. She had her head bowed and her hands over her eyes, crying because she missed Jesus and because she did not fully understand what had happened and why things had happened the way they had. I heard the Lord speak to her, and saw the moment Mary came to the realization that the person she was seeing and the man who was speaking to her, was in fact the Risen Lord.

I saw her stand and reach out to hug Him, and heard the Lord as He told her, "Touch me not, for I have not yet ascended to my Father." I witnessed the complete joy and happiness in her face and manner as the Lord instructed her to go and tell others that He had risen, that He was a resurrected being, and that she had personally seen Him and spoken with Him.

I watched as Mary ran as fast as she could to the house of her friends, encountering people along the way and anxiously telling them what she had experienced and knew. I witnessed their excitement at receiving the news, and I watched as word spread among the people.

I witnessed Christ appearing to many others, and saw their varied reactions as they learned for themselves that He was the Risen Lord. I learned once again, that without a doubt, Christ overcame physical death. I know this. I witnessed this. After Christ was resurrected, I witnessed the resurrection of many others as well.

I know that because of the Atonement, everyone born on this earth will be resurrected (see 1 Corinthians 15:21-22). There is no doubt in my mind that this will happen. Just as Jesus was resurrected, our spirits will be reunited with our bodies.

It was made clear to me that the Savior's Atonement makes it possible for us to also overcome death of the spirit. Although all people will be resurrected, only those who accept the Atonement of Jesus Christ will be saved from spiritual death.

One of the ways we accept Christ's Atonement is by placing our faith in Him. Through faith, we repent of our sins, are baptized, receive the Holy Ghost, and learn to obey the Lord's commandments. Through faith we become faithful disciples of Jesus Christ. We can be forgiven and cleansed from all sin and prepare to return to live forever with our Heavenly Father.

Christ Visited the Nephites and Other Peoples

I saw what is recorded in the Book of Mormon—Jesus truly did visit the descendants of Lehi in the Americas. I witnessed many of the blessings and miracles performed by Christ. I witnessed Him embracing the children and administering to them and to the sick and afflicted. He cast out devils and raised the dead.

I witnessed Christ teaching the people and establishing His church on the American continent, in the same manner and organization in which it was organized in the Old World. I saw

Him ascending into the clouds upon leaving the people of the American continent.

I witnessed Christ visiting other nations, the islands of the sea, the Ten Tribes, and elsewhere. I witnessed Him performing the same kinds of miracles and teaching the same doctrines and principles, namely, the Gospel of Jesus Christ, including but not limited to teachings of the Plan of Salvation, the doctrines of the Atonement and about the Resurrection. I witnessed as He traveled the Heavens and the earth, appearing before vast multitudes of people, teaching and organizing His Gospel upon the earth and in the Spirit World.

I witnessed as He again taught them about the importance of baptism by immersion for the remission of sins, and of the power of the Holy Ghost, who is the third member of the Godhead. I listened as I heard Him teach that the way to know the truth of all things is through the power of the Holy Ghost.

I heard Him teach the people that through the Power of the Holy Ghost we can know all things, if we ask in faith. I heard Him teach the people that the Holy Ghost is the comforter, the revelator, and the voice of warning. It is through the power of the Holy Ghost that we can become truly converted and can come to know and understand the mysteries of God.

When it was time for Him to depart, I watched Him bid the people farewell. I witnessed Him ascend into the clouds with concourses of angels by His side. It was a glorious scene. Every knee was bowed. The people were left speechless. The impact of His visit lasted for generations.

The people became so righteous that there was no contention in the land for many years. The story of Christ's visit was passed down to future generations. Those who had witnessed this great event spent their lives testifying of Christ and of His divine role as the Savior of the world.

The Apostasy

I was shown that after a few centuries of light and truth, these nations all slipped into apostasy. The Dark Ages began, with persecutions of ancient Saints who suffered and died for Christ's sake.

My trials seemed so small in comparison to what I had witnessed through the centuries that I was deeply humbled and felt a strong need to repent for my lack of faith, my ingratitude, and my inability to fully appreciate all that the Lord had given me. I expressed this to John, and apologized for my selfishness and weakness. He expressed his love and essentially told me there was no need to apologize to him.

The Plan of Salvation

John reminded me once again of the Plan of Salvation as outlined by the Savior, and the power of the Atonement. He bore testimony of the Atonement's saving and healing power. He reminded me of the importance to repent of all things that are not in keeping with the Lord's ways, so that I could return and live with our Heavenly Father.

We talked about the importance of being obedient in all things. Specifically, that it is through obedience to God's commandments that we come to know Him, to become more like Him, and to ultimately receive all that the Father has promised us. (See Galatians 6:7; reap what we sow; see also James 1:22; be doers not merely hearers). Obedience is key. We develop faith, hope, and charity through obedience to the Lord's commandments.

Without obedience, we cannot obtain exaltation. Obedience is an eternal principle and it is the key to our eternal progression. Through obedience to God's laws, we find peace, happiness, safety and security. We are both physically and spiritually guided and protected when we obey the Lord.

John encouraged me to turn to the Lord in prayer and ask for His forgiveness, knowing that the price had already been paid in the Garden of Gethsemane and on the Cross. He also testified once again of the Lord's love for me, and for all of His children, and reminded me once again that we are not alone, that God is aware of each of us and knows us individually by name. His promises are sure. (See Proverbs 3:5-6.)

John talked once more about the Plan of Happiness, and how important it is that we make good choices. He urged me to think about the choices I had made, and those I would yet make, and to remember that our choices affect others. He reminded me that the choices we make every day either lead us toward or away from the light, and that depending on what choices we make, we are either on the Lord's side (the winning team), or on Satan's side.

There really is no middle ground. Either we choose to support God's Plan of Happiness, or we choose to fight against it. He also reminded me again that all of those spirits in the preexistence who had chosen to support the Lord's plan had been given the promise of inheriting a mortal body on the earth and had been clearly taught about the Plan of Happiness in the preexistence.

Satan is real and has many hosts of heaven that were cast out with him and who help him. I was shown that there are many different spirits who have been and would continue to try to confuse and misguide me. Their goal is to interfere in God's plan for us and to destroy us.

The Lord knows the End from the Beginning. It is we who are here to work out our own salvation through our own choices, and that through the power of the Atonement, all mankind may be saved through faith. John reminded me about many of the things I had previously been taught: That through the grace and mercy of Jesus Christ, you can become clean from sin and enjoy peace of conscience. You can become worthy to live in our Heavenly Father's presence after this life.

He reminded me of the importance of certain ordinances while on the earth, including the need to be baptized by the proper authority, and partaking of the sacrament. We talked again about the Plan of Salvation and how it is God's plan for the happiness of His children, centered on the Atonement of Jesus Christ.

I was shown more about the Creation and the Fall, and about historical events that had happened on the earth. We talked about Christ's suffering in the Garden of Gethsemane and on the cross, so that all mankind might be saved, if they would repent and come unto Him. We also discussed the miracle of Christ's resurrection and how that made it possible for each of God's children to one day also be resurrected.

John clarified some things about Heaven. He talked to me about where we go when we die, and what happens to those who either never knew of Christ, or for some reason they did not accept Christ while living on the earth. He confirmed what I had been taught—after we are resurrected, we will go before God to be judged according to our works and the desires of our hearts. He further explained the Degrees of Glory—known as the Celestial, Terrestrial, and Telestial kingdoms. He told me about each of the kingdoms, and how there are actually many degrees of glory within each Degree of Glory.

John reassured me that for those who die in their sins, particularly for those who commit suicide, all is not forgotten, nor is all hope lost. There is a way prepared for them to come back as well. It is a difficult path, especially because it is much more difficult to overcome the weaknesses of the flesh without a mortal body, but there is a way. We should never lose faith or hope for ourselves or our loved ones who have strayed.

John asked me if I was ready to continue on with our journey. I replied that I was, and I followed him out of the library. On our way out, as we were walking down the steps to the front of the library, he again greeted some more people that he knew. He introduced us. A little while later, I looked up and noticed a group of men dressed in white robes standing in a group conversing.

I thought to myself that they looked familiar. John asked me if I knew who they were. I paused, and then responded that I did in fact recognize who they were. They were men of great importance both in the Councils of Heaven, as well as when they lived on earth.

The Founding Fathers

We walked on, and as we walked we came to a gathering of men. As we approached, John indicated that there were some men he wanted me to meet. I followed, anxious to find out who they were and what it was John wanted me to do. The men looked up as we approached, and smiling at us and to one another, they greeted us warmly.

Within a matter of moments, I was introduced to the group. Most of the people were unfamiliar to me; however, there were a few I met who were unmistakable and unforgettable. I quickly learned that I was in the presence of a few of the Founding Fathers, and other leaders of our nation.

I also learned that some of the men present had served as soldiers during the Revolutionary and Civil Wars. I learned that a few in the group had served during World War I and others during World War II.

I had the honor and privilege of meeting and visiting with a few of these men for a brief period of time. The purpose of my visit was discussed, and it was agreed upon that once I returned to my life on earth, I would do the best I could to tell the world the truth about our great country, the importance of the Constitution, and the true facts pertaining to Christopher Columbus, and the Founding Fathers.

Benjamin Franklin, John Adams, Thomas Jefferson, and Christopher Columbus were greatly concerned about the lies that have been and continue to be told about them and others.

They were not necessarily concerned for themselves, they were concerned about the deceit that has occurred which has blinded many and caused so many on the earth to be led astray. They were concerned about the wickedness and immorality of the people of the world, but they were particularly upset about the corruption of the American government and its citizens.

I listened as they voiced their concerns, and they essentially told me the true state of the Union and the dire consequences that would come upon the American people if they did not "wake up and get their act together."

These men knew of the importance of the Constitution of the Unites States, and they bore testimony to me of the divine role this country has played and of its foreordained mission.

The Importance of the Family

They reiterated the importance of the family, and bore testimony of its divine origin. They emphasized the fact that from the beginning Satan has fought against the family and has done and will continue to do all he can to destroy the family. It was made very clear to me that Satan uses many tactics to accomplish this goal.

These great leaders also talked to me about the significant responsibility we each have to uphold the laws of the land as outlined in the Constitution. It was made clear to me that unless we as a people repent of our evil ways and turn to God, there will be devastating consequences that will sweep across the nation. As long as the people are righteous, God protects them.

When people become wicked, idolatrous, rebellious, and lovers of selves more than lovers of God, they cut themselves off from

His presence and suffer the consequences. It was shown that the family is central to Heavenly Father's plan for the eternal destiny of His children. All human beings have been created in the image of God. Each individual has a divine nature and destiny.

The divine plan of happiness enables family relationships to continue into the eternities. Sacred ordinances and covenants available in the temple make it possible for God's children to learn and progress and to one day return to His presence. They make it possible for families to be united eternally.

The family is ordained of God. Marriage between a man and a woman is ordained of God. The family is essential to God's eternal plan of happiness.

It is no coincidence that we are born into the families we come to. From the very beginning the Lord designed it so that the family unit is essential to our salvation.

Satan and his minions know how essential the family is to God's eternal plan. They know that it is through these family ties that we learn to grow and develop. They know that in part it is our ancestors who serve as a shield and a protection to us.

They know that our family members beyond the veil work as ministering angels. They know that if they can hurt and destroy marriages and families, then they can successfully injure God's children and attack the heart.

Even from the very beginning, Satan and his minions have sought to destroy the family. From the days of Adam, Noah, Abraham, Moses and throughout all generations of time, the adversary's main objective has been to attack the family. Satan and those who follow him know that if they can successfully injure the family then they have in some measure succeeded in their wicked plans.

It is imperative that we do all we can to protect the family. It is critical that we recognize the role we play now and in the eternities.

It is important that we do all in our power to defend marriage and family as ordained by God. No matter the consequences, we need to stand for truth and righteousness. We need to take a firm stand and be willing to defend our faith and our families.

CHAPTER FIVE

The Book of Records

We left the library courtyard, walking down another street we had not yet been on. I followed John into another large building. As we entered, he told me he was going to show me several important things, and to pay close attention. As we stood in what appeared to be an entryway, it seemed a scene opened up before me. I was shown a variety of settings, some very similar to each other, and others very unique.

I saw cottages, farms, villages, cities, a variety of landscapes and scenery, small homes, medium-sized homes, and huge mansions. I learned that what I was being shown was a small sample of what was "available" or "possible" for me, once I passed on from mortality to the Spirit World. The understanding came to me that I could choose for myself. I could have whatever would make me happy.

I followed John down a large corridor. We passed many rooms with closed doors. The ceilings were very tall. John took me into one of the rooms, and inside from floor to ceiling were books. They were of fine workmanship and appeared to be made of high quality materials.

John walked over to one of the book shelves. He reached up and took a book off one of the shelves at what appeared to be about six feet high. I know this because I am five foot ten inches tall, and the place from which he took the book was slightly higher than the top of my head.

He told me that he was going to show me some parts of the Book of Life, which is like the universe's super computer system. These records contain every deed, word, thought, feeling, intent and action that has ever occurred at any time in the history of the world.

He opened the book and directed my full attention to the page he opened. It listed my name. He showed me specific passages. It was a book of records about MY life. He told me when it mentions in the scriptures about the book of records, this is part of what the Lord is referring to. Although it was a book, it was as if I was watching video footage of these events.

The Book of Life contains the entire history of the earth, including every person since the beginning of the Creation. It connects each one of us to one another. Information about the Book of Life is found throughout the Old and New Testaments. It is not simply a book about the past. It also includes the present and possibilities for the future.

The Latter-day Restoration of the Gospel

As I read the book, my attention was soon drawn to the events that led to the restoration of The Church of Jesus Christ in the latter days. I was shown many of the events that led to the pilgrims settling in the Americas.

I watched as Jamestown was settled. I saw the meager beginnings of the new settlers, many of whom were seeking religious freedom. I witnessed the travels of those on the Mayflower and other ships as the people came to the Americas in hope of a better life.

I saw some of their interactions with the Native Americans, and was shown the first Thanksgiving. I saw villages and towns built, and people gathering in worship. I was shown scenes from the early Quaker and Puritan settlements, as well as those of many other denominations.

In time, it was made clear to me that there was a wide variety of religious interest and that there was great confusion and competition between the sects. Some were drawn to one group, and others were drawn to another. Preachers taught their own interpretations from the Bible, and doctrines often clashed between groups. Divisions arose and often feelings between friends and family became tense.

Many of these individuals who were seeking knowledge and religion began to judge and mistreat one another due to their misunderstandings. This went on for some time, and seemed to increase and intensify. It was not uncommon for family divisions to occur as a result of the differences in opinion.

These scenes saddened me, as I came to the realization that the adversary had done all in his power to deceive and distract, and to divide families. What had once brought many of the early settlers to the Americas—a desire for religious freedom—now caused more grief and sorrow. It set the stage, however, for the restoration of the Church of Jesus Christ upon the earth.

Joseph's Smith's First Vision

I witnessed a young teenage boy, Joseph Smith, talking to his parents, particularly to his mother, about the things he was hearing and witnessing amongst the people in his small town. He asked her what she thought of it all, and if she believed that God had a true church. He asked her if she felt any of the congregations in their town taught the truth, as written in the King James Bible.

They had many discussions about this topic, and Joseph was very inquisitive and determined to learn for himself. His mother, Lucy Mack Smith, responded in faith that she did not know for sure which church was true, but she did feel God's love. She reminded Joseph of God's love and encouraged him to study it out on his own by continuing to read and study the Bible. She encouraged him to pray.

Joseph Smith studied the Bible daily. He sought answers and he read fervently. Like so many others, Joseph was seeking truth, but he was very confused. One day, while reading the Bible, he came across some verses in scripture that had profound impact on him. I watched as he read in James 1:5, "If any of you lack wisdom, let him ask of God, that giveth to all men liberally, and upbraideth not; and it shall be given him."

As Joseph read this verse of scripture, and continued to read and study further, he eventually came to the conclusion that he needed to act on the knowledge he had been given. He realized that he could remain confused, or he could ask God in faith for answers to his sincere questions. The Holy Ghost testified to him of the truth of the scriptures he had read, and prompted him to take action.

Joseph decided to ask God himself for the truth, and to ask the Lord if any of the churches he had attended were His true church. Joseph had been taught the importance of baptism, and he desired to be baptized into the true Church of Christ.

I watched as Joseph walked from his home, across a meadow and into a nearby forest. He walked into the forest for some time before stopping to rest. He found a small clearing in the trees and sat down on a nearby log. In great thought and contemplation, he mustered his faith and courage and finally knelt in prayer.

Despite the overwhelming powers of the adversary, who not only sought to obscure his ability to pray, but had set out to destroy him, Joseph mustered all of his strength and power and called upon God to deliver him from the darkness that had enveloped him. I witnessed this struggle and saw with my own eyes as I was shown how things played out.

True to Joseph's own account, just as he was ready to give up in despair and total exhaustion—just at that moment, to his great alarm—he saw a pillar of light above him. I watched as this great light increased in size and brightness. It was a brilliant light, and it completely dispelled the darkness.

The light rested upon Joseph and as it did so, Joseph's entire frame and figure changed from one of great despair and exhaustion to that of complete calm and awe. In the light stood two beings whose brightness and glory were so incredible, there is no way I could describe the intensity. I recognized them immediately for who they were, and I witnessed one say to Joseph, addressing him by name, "This is my beloved son. Hear Him!" I recognized that the one who had spoken was God the Father, and he was referencing our Savior Jesus Christ.

I watched and listened as they talked to Joseph about what he knew to be true, what he felt in his heart to be true, and as they taught him what was actually true. I heard Joseph express his sincere desires to know the truth, and I heard him ask the Lord which, of all of the churches, he should join, that he might be baptized and dedicate his life to the Lord.

I heard them tell Joseph that although many of the churches taught good things, none of them contained the fullness of the Gospel of Jesus Christ. I heard the Lord tell him that he should join none of the churches.

They also told him about the Plan of Salvation, about the purpose of the Atonement, and about God's great eternal plan for each of His children. I heard them speak of the importance of being baptized by immersion for the remission of sins, by one having proper authority. I heard them speak to him about the importance of personal revelation, or direction from the Lord.

They briefly taught Joseph about the organization of the church, and how in times past the Lord had established churches that were organized with prophets and apostles who held the priesthood of God, or the authority to speak and act in the name of God to lead His children.

I heard them speak of the importance of prophets and how those who follow the prophets receive the blessings God has promised. I heard them explain to Joseph that those who reject the gospel and God's prophets lose those blessings and distance themselves from God. I watched and heard them explain that those who reject the prophets and abandon their commitment to follow God are in a condition called apostasy.

I listened as they explained and clarified about what had happened on the earth in previous dispensations, which had led to the great apostasy and the priesthood being taken from the earth. I heard them speak about the veil of darkness that was about to be lifted from the world, and about some of the role that Joseph would play in bringing about a great work. I heard them express their great love for Joseph, and for all people, and I watched as they expressed their sincere desires for Joseph to understand and comprehend the messages he was receiving, and those he would yet receive.

I witnessed and heard them tell Joseph not to fear the adversary, or those who might seek to do harm. I heard them promise him protection and additional guidance. I listened to them explain that he would receive additional light and knowledge, and heard them encourage him to continue to have faith and to be obedient to the commandments. They promised him that he would not be alone, and they explained that other messengers would attend him in the future.

I saw and felt the inexplicable joy and relief on Joseph's face as they explained all of these things and more to him in the grove of trees. I heard them bid him farewell, with the promise of great things if he was faithful and obedient to the commandments of God. I watched as they departed and drew up into the heavens.

Upon their leaving, I saw Joseph lying on the ground in

complete exhaustion. I saw him fall upon his face, overcome with tears and strong emotion, as he came to the realization of what had just occurred. He tried to comprehend all that he had just experienced, and he prayed in gratitude to God for the answers to his prayers. I then saw him quietly, reverently, peacefully walk out of the grove and back to his home.

He entered his home and went to the nearby fireplace. He leaned against it, fatigued and in deep contemplation. His loving mother, sensing that something was weighing upon her son, asked if something was wrong with him. He responded that he was fine, that everything was all right. He then told her that he had learned for himself that Presbyterianism was not true.

Moments later, I saw him retire to his bedroom, where he collapsed on his bed in complete exhaustion. Later, I witnessed him tell his mother, and then both of his parents, about what he had experienced. I listened as he later told his brothers and sisters who lived in the home. They were very supportive of Joseph, and did the best they could to make sense of what he was trying to tell them. Joseph's parents reacted with love and kindness.

I watched as Joseph, in his innocence and excitement, tried to share his experience with a Methodist preacher, and with others in whom he came in contact. It was heartbreaking to see their reactions. Not only were they not receptive to the message, they condemned Joseph and told him that it was all of the devil, saying there were no such things as visions or revelations in those days. They said that all such things had ceased with the apostles, and that there would never be any more of them.

To Joseph's dismay, he soon found that this was the common reaction to his story, and he found himself at the center of great persecution and ridicule. Although just a young teenage boy, he found that professors of religion, preachers, and people of all denominations were against him.

Despite the persecution, Joseph knew without a doubt that

what he had experienced in the grove that day was of God. He knew that the Lord had answered his prayers and he knew that he had beheld a vision. I personally witnessed some of this persecution, and I heard some of the awful things said to him.

With these scenes that I witnessed, I felt some of the intense pain that Joseph must have felt at that time. It was soul crushing. It brought me to tears.

It was evident that the adversary knew who Joseph Smith was, even as a young boy. He knew what Joseph was capable of even before Joseph himself consciously knew. Satan knew that Joseph's foreordained mission was to help restore the Church of Jesus Christ to the earth. He knew that Joseph was a future prophet of God, called to usher in the fullness of times in the last dispensation, as had been prophesied in the scriptures. Satan and his minions did all they could to stir up controversy and to stop Joseph from fulfilling his foreordained mission.

Visits with Moroni

I witnessed that three years after the First Vision, Joseph Smith received a visit from a heavenly messenger named Moroni, who was the last Nephite prophet. He had buried the Gold Plates in the Hill Cumorah in 421 A.D., and he had returned as a resurrected being to help prepare Joseph to receive them and translate them into what would be known as the Book of Mormon.

I witnessed this first appearance of Moroni to Joseph one night, after he had offered a heartfelt prayer of gratitude and made supplication to the Lord in asking God to forgive him for the error of his ways. I heard Joseph ask in faith for a manifestation from the spirit, that he might know his standing before the Lord, and that he might have further light and knowledge pertaining to his purpose and mission in life.

I saw the light descend and the brightness of the room increase as the angel Moroni, dressed in a white robe, appeared to Joseph. I watched as Joseph spent the majority of the night listening to Moroni explain about the Book of Mormon records, the history of his people. Moroni also told of the important role that Joseph would play in bringing to pass the purposes of the Lord.

Moroni told Joseph that the Book of Mormon records contained the Gospel of Jesus Christ, and a record of some of the people who had lived on the American continent. I listened as Moroni explained that the Book of Mormon would serve as a second witness of the Savior. It would be instrumental in bringing God's children to the truthfulness of the restored gospel. I also listened as Moroni taught Joseph from the scriptures. He explained that the day had come for the priesthood to be restored by the hand of Elijah the prophet before the great and dreadful day of the Lord.

I heard the angel Moroni quote the scripture in Malachi which prophesies, "And he shall plant in the hearts of the children the promises made to the fathers, and the hearts of the children shall turn to their fathers. If it were not so, the whole earth would be utterly wasted at his coming."

I listened and heard the angel quote many other scriptures from the Bible, pertaining to our day. I heard Moroni tell Joseph about the records, and where he could find them.

I watched him open a vision to Joseph, where he showed him exactly what the records looked like, and where they were to be found. I saw him point to the destination and give specific instructions pertaining to the messages he was receiving.

Moroni visited with Joseph two more times that night, sharing essentially the same message each time. Shortly before the sun rose, Moroni departed, leaving Joseph with strict counsel and guidance in reference to his mission and the knowledge he had gained.

I witnessed as the next day Joseph was working in the field with his father chopping wood. I saw the look of complete exhaustion on Joseph's face, and I saw his father dismiss him from his day's work, to go home and rest.

I watched as Joseph walked back toward home, and just as he was about to cross over a fence into their nearby property, Joseph collapsed onto the ground. I saw him laying there, as if in a deep sleep. I witnessed the angel Moroni come visit him again in that green field, and I heard the angel talk to Joseph in great detail, reminding him again of what he had learned the previous night. I watched Joseph regain his strength and return home, going directly to his bed and falling asleep, his body so desperately needing rest.

I later saw Joseph walk a great distance to the Hill Cumorah to the exact location he had been shown. I watched as Joseph followed the instructions he had been given, and as he rolled away the large stone that was covering the place the records had been stored.

I watched in amazement as Joseph viewed the records for the first time, attended by the angel Moroni, who met with him there. On that first visit to the Hill Cumorah, Moroni strictly forbade Joseph from touching the plates or anything that accompanied them, saying the time had not come for him to translate them.

Later I witnessed Joseph's progression over the next four years as the time drew near for him to obtain the plates, prior to taking on the duty and responsibility of translating and protecting the records.

Witnessing these events left me with an absolute confirmation that Joseph really talked with Moroni and that he was given the gold plates by an angel of God. I was left with an absolute sure knowledge that Joseph Smith was and is a true prophet of God, and that the work he performed while in mortality was and is part of God's eternal plan.

Translating the Plates

I saw Joseph Smith translating the Gold Plates, with his friend Oliver Cowdery working as scribe. I was also shown many scenes where Joseph and his wife Emma worked on the translation. I had always believed this since childhood and had faith that Joseph Smith was a prophet, but at the time, I was really struggling with my testimony of Joseph Smith and had prayed for a confirmation that he had really seen God and translated the plates.

Upon viewing these scenes, it was made absolutely clear to me that Joseph Smith did in fact translate these sacred records, now known in modern day as The Book of Mormon. My faith and knowledge of the restoration of the Gospel of Jesus Christ increased as I came to a greater understanding of the Lord's plan.

I saw for myself that God had foreordained this great man and had called him as a modern day prophet of God. There is no way on earth that Joseph Smith could have accomplished what he did, without the divine assistance he received. He had very little formal schooling, yet he miraculously translated entire records of scripture that surpass the knowledge, comprehension and understanding of the world's finest scholars. It is truly a miraculous work and a wonder.

The Priesthood is Restored

I witnessed John the Baptist giving Oliver Cowdery and Joseph Smith the Aaronic Priesthood. From this I learned with surety that one must be ordained to the necessary priesthood by one having authority before he can administer the ordinances of the gospel.

It was also confirmed to me that the Aaronic Priesthood holds the keys of the ministering of angels, the gospel of repentance, and baptism by immersion for the remission of sins. It was also made very clear to me that this priesthood will never again be taken from the earth, and while it is divine authority from God, its administration is limited.

Peter, James and John Appear

I was shown that Peter, James and John, apostles of the Lord Jesus Christ, did in fact bestow the Melchizedek Priesthood upon Joseph Smith and Oliver Cowdery.

This Melchizedek Priesthood, including the holy apostleship as promised by John the Baptist, gave them authority to organize the church and the Kingdom of God upon the earth in this dispensation. As has been prophesied in scripture for thousands of years, God has in fact restored His church here upon the earth, with all of the principles and ordinances of the Gospel contained therein.

Emma Smith

I saw Emma Smith, Joseph's wife and first President of the Relief Society, gather hymns for the making of hymnals. I watched as she worked diligently to gather and collect words and music that would edify the Saints. This increased my testimony of the importance and the power of music in worship. It was remarkable to witness the early Saints as they sang praises to the Most High, and as they endured great hardship because of opposition to their beliefs.

I recognized Emma Smith and her great contributions to her husband, as well as to the church, and I witnessed her many sacrifices in helping to build up the Kingdom of God on the earth. It was made clear to me that she is an elect lady, and that the Lord has reserved a special place in His Kingdom for her. She was a woman of great faith and obedience, and her supportive role to Joseph made it possible for Joseph to complete the mission the Lord gave him.

Emma endured countless devastating trials and tribulations, yet she spent her life with Joseph in complete sacrifice and service to others. She was indeed a godly woman who overcame awful situations. Witnessing scenes from Emma's life gave me a greater appreciation for her, and provided a firm testimony of the importance of the Relief Society.

It also strengthened my own resolve to sacrifice and serve wherever and whenever I can. It is through service and sacrifice that we truly learn to love the Lord and love our fellowman.

The Kirtland Temple

I witnessed the appearances of Elias and Elijah the prophets in the Kirtland Temple, and the appearances of others as recorded in scripture. The sealing ordinances were restored, with the same blessings promised to Abraham.

This solidified my testimony of Joseph Smith and Oliver Cowdery really having these powers restored to them in the Kirtland Temple. It also solidified my testimony of eternal families and of sealing powers, endowments, and baptisms for the dead in temple work, as is taught in the scriptures.

These visits, in conjunction with others, brought about the fullness of the gospel in the latter days. It was clearly communicated to me yet again of the divine truth of Joseph Smith being a prophet of God and of the restoration of the Gospel of Jesus Christ upon the earth in the latter days.

The Haun's Mill Massacre

I was shown scenes regarding the Haun's Mill Massacre. Jacob Haun was a miller from New York. He came to eastern Missouri and established a settlement. Although he was not a member of the LDS Church, several LDS families settled in Haun's Mill. There were twelve families in Haun's Mill and another 75 families in the surrounding areas. Joseph Smith had counseled the Saints to gather and settle in Far West, Missouri, not far from this settlement.

Due to hostilities from the local people, Jacob Haun traveled to Far West and visited with Joseph Smith. He asked Joseph what he felt they should do about the impending threat. Joseph told him to tell the Saints that they should leave Haun's Mill and join the Saints in Far West. Rather than relaying this message to the Saints, Jacob instead told them that Joseph had said it would be fine for them to stay where they were and do the best they could for self-protection.

The people of Haun's Mill were concerned about their safety. Missouri leaders from Livingston came to Haun's Mill under the pretense of coming to some sort of a "peace settlement." They convinced most of the settlers to give up their arms in a show of mutual cooperation. Unfortunately this was just a set up. Their real purpose was to disarm the people so there would be less resistance when they attacked the settlement.

Prior to the attack, approximately 200 individuals painted their faces to avoid being identified. Then they stormed the settlement, shooting at every man, woman and child they saw. It was truly a bloody massacre.

I was shown some of the importance of what occurred at Haun's Mill and how it relates to our day. Mainly, the Saints of Haun's Mill had been given counsel and direction to settle in Far West. They had later been told to vacate the area, but the people did not receive the real message from the prophet. They were deceived not only by Jacob Haun, but also later by the Missouri mobs.

Had the Saints settled in Far West as originally instructed, they would have been protected. Had Jacob Haun given them the true message to leave Haun's Mill and join the other Saints in Far West, they would have been gathered together and would have been protected. Had the Saints left Haun's Mill when counseled to do so, this terrible massacre would have been avoided.

This story is sad, but true. I was shown that there are great lessons that can be learned from their experiences. I saw that in our day, many of us will face similar circumstances. I was shown that those who failed to listen to and heed the counsel of the living prophet and apostles paid a very high price for their choices. Those who followed the prophet were given additional protection and guidance. This story serves as a warning to us all as a modern-day example of the importance of heeding the counsel of the living prophet.

The Saints Fleeing Persecution in Missouri

I was shown other scenes from the days of the early Saints, and witnessed the persecution and mistreatment of the early Mormon settlers. I saw the massacres that occurred, and I watched speechless as families were torn apart, women and children were violated, and people were murdered in cold blood.

While Joseph Smith was held captive in Liberty Jail for several months, the homes of members were burned and I saw more of the awful treatment the Saints received from mobs. I was also given a close up view of the horrendous conditions that Joseph and Hyrum and others in their party experienced while being held captive illegally in Liberty Jail.

Witnessing these horrendous scenes gave me a different perspective on my own trials at the time, which although they were very difficult for me, they felt like nothing in comparison to what I was being shown.

This experience yet again reminded me of how blessed I was, and that although we may suffer in this life due to the choices of others, the Lord is aware of us. Wicked perpetrators do not escape justice. The blood of the innocents cries from the dust and one day those who have committed these awful crimes will pay for their abhorrent acts.

It was yet again made clear to me that those who have gone before us are very much alive in the Spirit World. We are not alone. There are angels all around us. It was also made very clear to me that just as the followers of Christ in days past endured great trials, tribulation, and persecution for Christ's sake, we too will be called upon to endure many difficult things.

It was made known to me how important it is and will be for me and for others to stand in holy places. It was made clear to me regarding the need and importance of standing for truth and righteousness, no matter the opposition and no matter the consequences.

Some will be called upon to fight for our freedoms. Many will be called upon to fight for our religious freedom and for the Constitution of the United States of America. Although many will lose their lives in the battles for freedom, they will gain a great reward in the hereafter. I was shown that although there will be many casualties, ultimately the Lord's people will win the fight. God will prevail and the righteous will overcome the wicked.

The Nauvoo Temple Being Built

I saw many scenes regarding the building of the city of Nauvoo and of the great temple that was originally built there. I witnessed the hard work, sacrifice and dedication of the early pioneers as they worked tirelessly on this temple. They were anxious to build the temple so that they could perform important temple ordinances for their deceased loved ones, as well as for themselves.

I became very much aware of the importance of baptisms for the dead, and it was confirmed to me how important it is for us to do our part in researching our ancestral lines, doing family history work, and taking our family names to the temple.

Joseph Smith Martyred in Carthage Jail

I saw Joseph and his brother Hyrum murdered in Carthage Jail. This was in conjunction with what I was shown about the Saints fleeing west. As one can imagine, these scenes were absolutely horrific.

Upon viewing these events, I yet again became very emotional. There are not words to describe the massacre that occurred on that fateful day. It was horrendous. The murderous actions of that wicked mob still haunt me to this day.

I gain comfort in knowing that one day justice will be paid and the truth will be made known to all people. Those who have suffered for Christ's sake, especially those who have been martyred, have and will continue to find peace in the hereafter.

They have not died in vain. The Lord is over all, and He has prepared mansions in heaven for the righteous. Those who have lost their lives in defending truth and righteousness have sealed their place in the eternal kingdoms of our Lord. Their reward is great and God has and will continue to fulfill all of the promises He has made to His children.

The Exodus from Nauvoo

I witnessed the Saints fleeing for their lives and the burning of the Nauvoo Temple. I saw the Saints traveling across the plains, eventually settling in what is now known as the state of Utah.

At this point I also saw scenes about my pioneer ancestors. I watched as thousand of Saints crossed the plains in wagons and with handcarts.

I saw many of the heartaches, sacrifices, and difficulties the early pioneers endured. Witnessing their resolve and dedication strengthened my testimony of the gospel and my knowledge that families are forever.

The Mormon Battalion

I was shown scenes leading up to and pertaining to the gathering of the Mormon Battalion. I was shown how they were like the stripling warriors spoken of in the Book of Mormon.

It was made known to me that there will come a time in our day when we will be called upon to serve and sacrifice in the same manner. There will be a modern "battalion" in the last days. As mentioned previously, some will be required to give their lives for the freedom of the United States and the gospel.

The Establishment of Salt Lake City

I clearly remember being shown scenes about the early pioneers reaching the Salt Lake Valley. Brigham Young truly had been shown that Salt Lake City was "the place." I watched as he was directed by the spirit in leading the people to Utah, and as he chose the spot for the building of the Salt Lake Temple.

I was shown details about the stories that have been told of millions of crickets attacking the fields of the early pioneers, and how thousands of seagulls "came to the rescue" by descending upon the crickets.

I saw miracles performed in the lives of many, and I witnessed healings, protections, and other spiritual manifestations among the people. Faith was tested. Faith was strengthened.

The people grew in knowledge, strength, and wisdom as they followed the teachings of a living prophet and obeyed the Lord's commandments.

Building the Salt Lake Temple

I was shown various scenes regarding the building of the great Salt Lake Temple. The building of the temple took approximately 40 years to complete. Great sacrifice, hard work, faith, and dedication were required.

It required an intense level of commitment and determination from all involved. There were many long, tiring days, and times were difficult, but the faithful believers did all in their power to build that glorious structure.

Although the early pioneers were very poor and had few material possessions of their own, they gave not only of their time and talents willingly, they also gave what little money and material possessions they had to help contribute to the building of the temple.

The materials and labor were of the finest workmanship in that day. No shortcuts were taken. This was a noble house of worship, dedicated to the Most High. Although there were many who worked on the temple who were never able to see the final fruits of their labor while in the flesh, millions have now received their temple ordinances and have been the recipients of their years of sacrifice and dedication.

Founding Fathers Appear in the St. George Temple

I was shown that Christopher Columbus and the Founding Fathers appeared to President Wilford Woodruff in the St. George Temple.

Most of the men were ordained as Elders, but five men were ordained to the office of High Priest: Benjamin Franklin, Christopher Columbus, John Wesley (Methodist founder), George Washington (first U.S. president), and Lord Horatio Nelson (an English explorer).

Temple work was completed for all of these men, as well as for dozens of other men and women well-known throughout history, some of which include: Americus Vespucius, James Madison, Andrew Jackson, Henry Clay, Abigail Smith (wife of John Adams), and Sarah Ford (wife of Samuel Johnson).

Lorenzo Snow

I was taught the importance of paying tithing. I was shown scenes from the days when President Lorenzo Snow was the prophet of the Church.

There was famine in the land, and food and water were scarce. It had not rained for days. The Church and the people were very poor. The early pioneers had endured much and they were struggling to survive. Many had come to President Snow in desperation, seeking help to pay their bills and provide for their families.

President Snow inquired of the Lord and asked Him to spare the people and to answer their faithful prayers. The Lord told President Snow that the people needed to pay a tithe of 10 percent of their income—whether that be monetarily, or through the giving of 10 percent of their crops, their eggs, milk, or flocks— whatever they could that was an increase. The Lord told President Snow that if the people were faithful and followed through in obedience to the law of tithing, then He would send rain.

He promised the Prophet that in time the Church and the people would become a wealthy people. God directed President Snow to teach this principle to the early Saints, and to testify to them and to all people about the Law of Tithing, as taught in the scriptures. He promised them that if obedient to this law, He would pour out His blessings. He reminded President Snow to teach the people what is stated in the Book of Mormon:

"Bring ye all the tithes into the storehouse, that there may be meat in my house; and prove me now herewith saith the Lord of Hosts, if I will not open you the windows of heaven, and pour you out a blessing that there shall not be room enough to receive it. And I will rebuke the devourer for your sakes, and he shall not destroy the fruits of your ground; neither shall your vine cast her fruit before the time in the fields, saith the Lord of Hosts. And all nations shall call you blessed, for ye shall be a delightsome land, saith the Lord of Hosts." (3 Nephi 24:10-12)

The Growth of the Church Across the World

I witnessed various scenes from the history of the Church of Jesus Christ of Latter-day Saints in the decades that followed. I saw that over time, the church grew exponentially. What started out as a small group of faithful truth-seekers led to millions of people learning about the restored Gospel of Jesus Christ.

I saw the increased sacrifices of the early Saints, as men left their families to go to distant lands and preach the Gospel. I witnessed thousands of people in Europe and other countries as they were taught the gospel by these righteous missionaries and leaders. I heard and listened as these missionaries bore witness of the truthfulness of the restored Gospel, and as they prayerfully and diligently were guided by the spirit to those who were seeking answers.

I watched as these truth-seekers recognized and embraced the truth. I saw the tears on their faces as the Holy Ghost bore witness to their souls that Jesus is the Christ and that He had in fact appeared to Joseph Smith. I heard them sing praises to God, in thanks and gratitude, as they developed their own testimonies and came to an understanding of the principles and ordinances of the gospel.

I watched as the faithful left the luxuries of home and family and traveled across the seas to an unknown land, to gather with those of like minds, in many cases leaving behind all they had. I witnessed them coming by boat to the American continent, in response to the call to gather in the Rocky Mountains. I watched as many of them crossed the plains in dire circumstances. I saw children born, and many die along the way.

I saw that as time went on, just as they had been promised,

the people began to flourish in the land. I witnessed the increased building of temples and churches across the world, and the increased efforts in missionary work. I witnessed the gathering of the Saints to hear the words of prophets and apostles as they sought truth and divine guidance in their lives.

I saw that eventually the gospel was taught in all lands and to all people. I witnessed the conversions and baptisms of people from all over the world, and I saw the peace, joy, and happiness that radiated from them as they increased in faith and obedience.

The Hastening of the Work

As mentioned previously, I was shown many scenes relating to missionary work. I was shown scenes of missionary work not only on the earth, but also some of that which has taken place and will continue to take place in the Spirit World. In the early days of the restored Church, many men were called to leave their families to travel throughout the United States, Canada, Europe, and other countries to preach the gospel.

As a result of these efforts, many traveled to America to gather with other members of the Church. Some stayed in their homelands. Branches and wards were established, and eventually stakes were set up. I witnessed the gathering of the people in different lands, and I watched as the missionary effort increased.

I saw thousands of young men and women, as well as senior missionaries, serving in various capacities throughout the world. I also witnessed the faith, obedience and service of thousands of faithful members of the Church as they served in their church callings, their families, and their communities. All of these efforts led to an increase in church membership. I witnessed the conversions, baptisms, and fellowship of thousands.

I was shown some of the humanitarian work that has been conducted by members of the Church. I saw great relief efforts as members throughout the world responded to the call to serve their fellowmen. I witnessed food, water, and other supplies being shipped to and dispersed to people in need. I witnessed the relief efforts of missionaries as well as regular members of the Church, as they responded to the needs of those in despair and desperation during and after natural disasters, war, disease, famine, and drought. I saw lives change. I witnessed the positive effects of the gospel on those who had embraced it.

I was shown that the missionary effort would increase substantially, and that there would be a great hastening of the work in the latter days. I was shown that the fruits of the spirit would be evident in the lives of the people. I witnessed many miracles, and I was shown that as time draws closer to the Second Coming of the Lord, even greater miracles will occur.

It was made very clear to me that those who have ears to hear and eyes to see will recognize the fruits of the spirit. They will also recognize the signs of the times all around them, and will do all in their power to spread the light of the gospel to their friends and family members.

Missionaries Called Home for a Time

It was made clear to me that there would come a point in time when missionaries would be called home, and formal missionary efforts would be stopped for a time. Due to the state of the world, prior to the Second Coming of the Lord, the Church would no longer send missionaries to foreign lands.

I was shown that this would occur after a huge increase in missionary efforts had occurred throughout the world, as a last and final attempt to help the Lord gather in His sheep and prepare the righteous for His coming. I was shown that later, 144,000 high priests, and in many cases, their wives, would again be called and set apart as special representatives of the Lord's Church, traveling to distant lands throughout the world, spreading the message of the Gospel to all of God's children.

At the same time, the City of Zion would be built up and the stakes of Zion would be strengthened. Those from the other side of the veil would assist in this great work, including the building of Zion, the gathering of the Lord's elect, and the establishment of the New Jerusalem on the American continent.

There have been and will continue to be great missionary efforts both on the earth and in the Spirit World. I was told and was shown that all of the Lord's children will be taught about Christ, about His Atonement, and about the Plan of Salvation.

Every child of God who has ever lived on the earth, or who will yet live on the earth, will be taught the full and complete Gospel of Jesus Christ. Every child of God will have to make a choice as to whether or not they would like to follow God's plan and continue to progress, or whether they will reject His plan and follow the adversary.

I was shown that there will one day be a final battle between those who follow Christ, and those who follow Satan. I was shown that the final battle will be fierce. I was shown that although there will be many who will fall, the majority of the righteous will rise up and face the opposition, with great faith and courage. I was shown that in the end, the Lord and His people will win.

Satan and those who follow him will be cast out forever, never to hurt and torment man again. God will be victorious. The righteous who have been obedient to the Lord's commands will receive the blessings the Father has promised His children from the beginning. I know this to be true. There is no doubt in my mind that these things will happen, and that the day will come when every knee will bow and every tongue confess that Jesus is the Christ, the Savior and Redeemer of the world.

CHAPTER SIX

Mansions in Heaven

John gently closed the Book of Life and placed it back on the shelf. He stood and beckoned for me to follow him. It seemed almost instantly we had left the earth and were in another world. It is here that I personally witnessed our Savior ministering to those who were in His presence.

Due to the sacredness of this experience, I will not share much about it here. I wish simply to testify that I know without a doubt we have a very kind and loving Heavenly Father and that His Only Begotten Son, Jesus Christ, is our older brother, our Savior, and our Redeemer. They love us more than we can even imagine. They have provided a wonderful plan for us.

I have seen them. I have seen the Throne of God and the Savior of Mankind standing on the right hand of God. I have seen concourses of angels singing praises to the Most High and shouting for joy as they have repented and been brought into the presence of our loving Heavenly Father. They are real. I know this without a doubt.

In the distance I saw a beautiful woman with dark hair, wearing a beautiful white dress, with a piece of pale blue fabric over her head and shoulders. She was surrounded by children, and by several other women who accompanied her. The children were tenderly holding her hands and touching her face.

She lovingly reached out to them and patted their tender cheeks. The children took turns sitting on her lap as she embraced them. It was made known to me that this beautiful sweet woman was cherished by God. Her beauty radiated. I learned that she is our Mother in Heaven.

I stood in awe of her for quite some time, cherishing the scene before me. I felt the love she had for those children, and I sensed her purity and goodness. She was truly the loveliest individual I have ever seen.

John just stood next to me quietly while I stared and tried to take in the beauty I was beholding. I watched her continue on through a few different parts of the city, and everywhere she went, the children begged to follow. Finally John told me we needed to continue.

Family Connections

I was shown specific people beyond the veil that I do not know, but it was made clear to me that they are my ancestors. I also saw some of my ancestors—my grandparents, some of my great aunts and uncles, great grandparents, along with Jeff's grandparents and some of his ancestors.

Missionary Work in the Spirit World

There are two main divisions in the Spirit World. They are known as Paradise and Spirit Prison. I was shown the importance of missionary work as it relates to all of God's children. I was shown that there are millions of people in Spirit Prison who have been and are being taught the Gospel of Jesus Christ. Many are waiting for their ordinances to be done so that they can cross over from Spirit Prison to Paradise.

When temple ordinances are done for those who have passed on from mortality, it provides them with the blessing and opportunity to progress in the Spirit World. Those who have had accepted the gospel in mortality enter Paradise when they die. Those who have not had an opportunity to hear the message of the gospel and who have not yet accepted Jesus Christ go to Spirit Prison upon death. The spirits in Paradise attend to those in Spirit Prison and encourage them to accept the gospel.

I was shown that as our ancestors accept the gospel and receive their ordinances performed on their behalf in the temple, they are able to continue progressing in the Spirit World. They increase in light and power. This in turn helps us here on earth in a very real and powerful way. It is our ancestors who usually serve as our ministering and guardian angels, and the more we help them, the more they can help us. We need each other to be able to continue to progress in this life and in the next.

Family History Work

I was shown the importance of doing family history work, and how it relates to temple work and the hereafter. We have a duty and obligation to our ancestors to research and record our family history, and where possible, to complete their ordinance work in the temple. Families really are forever.

Missionary work has been done and will continue to be done in the Spirit World. Our ancestors who have been baptized and have accepted Jesus Christ teach those on the other side who have not yet been given that opportunity.

They continue to receive further light and knowledge in the Spirit World. As I mentioned earlier, they are also able to give us greater help and protection from beyond the veil. In a very real way, we need each other.

Modern technology, particularly the use of computer technology, has significantly helped this process. As time has gone on and our technology has improved, we have been able to research and record names, dates, and documents from people of all generations all over the world. The Lord has blessed us with the means possible for us to be able to more quickly and efficiently do this important work. This in turn has provided temple blessings to millions of God's children who have been waiting to enter Paradise.

I saw that as time progressed into the future, the need for this work increased and continued. Much of what we do during the Millennium will be related to family history work, temple work and missionary work.

Ultimately all of God's children will be given the opportunity to hear and accept the gospel. All those who choose to follow Him will fight in the final battle against the Adversary and his minions after the Millennium, when Satan is once again loosed upon the earth for the very last time.

CHAPTER SEVEN

My Life Review

We soon left that area and came to a large building with a modern architectural design. We entered and passed through several large rooms. It seemed that everywhere I looked there were men and women busy at work. They smiled warmly in my direction as we passed by them.

John spoke to a few of them, explaining our purpose. They led us to a separate room away from the masses. I was instructed to wait for a moment, and told that they would be right with me. Suddenly the lighting in the room changed, and as it did, I began to notice that up on the walls there were several pictures beginning to appear before me.

In what looked to be dark blank picture frames, I began to see photos or snapshots of myself, beginning with me as an infant, going through different stages in my life, and leading up to the present day. Some of the pictures included members of my family—my parents, my siblings, my husband, my children, and my extended family.

My attention was directed to what looked like a large movie screen. In front of me I watched as scenes from my life appeared on the screen. It was as if I were watching a detailed movie of my life. At various points during the "movie," there were blanked out areas. I understood that these represented specific things in my life that I either had repented of, or still had need to repent of. Although there was no actual picture showing, specific visual representations came to my mind and I was left with a clear recollection of what those instances were in reference to and what I still needed to make right in my life. I was getting a "life review."

I will not go into more detail about this section of my tour, other than to share one example of something that was made known to me that I needed to repent of at the time. It was something that I had carried with me for many years. At the time of my NDE, I was 31 years old.

This incident I am referring to occurred during my junior year of high school. To my knowledge, I was the only living human being who knew of the circumstances surrounding this incident. I share it for two purposes: 1) to illustrate my point about our life reviews; and 2) to express my sincere apologies to this day, for the hurt and damage I caused another person.

I was a new driver. I had obtained my driver's license just three weeks prior. It was about 10 p.m., and I was on my way home from work and decided to stop at the grocery store to get something. I was tired after a long day at school and work, and I was in a hurry to get home.

I drove into the grocery store parking lot and went to pull into an empty parking spot. I pulled up to a small, older gold/grayish colored car, and as I did, I accidentally hit the front driver's side door of that car. I was horrified! I was afraid. I was worried. I did not want to get into trouble, and more importantly, I knew my parents did not have the money to bail me out. I knew I didn't have the money either.

In a complete panic, I looked around the parking lot and realized I was alone. I looked to see if anyone had seen me. I realized that no one had seen my blunder, and in fear I fled the scene. The entire way home I cried and felt awful. I couldn't believe I had been so careless. I knew that what I had done was wrong, but I let fear overcome me and keep me from making the right choice. I was a coward, and I was guilty of injuring someone I did not even know.

I was late getting home from work, so although I had several promptings to go back and make it right—to find the owner of the car and make restitution—due to my fears I ignored the promptings I received and went home.

I didn't tell a soul. I didn't tell my parents. I didn't tell a sibling. I didn't tell a single friend.

I tried to push the guilt aside and I prayed and asked the Lord to please forgive me. I felt His love and I felt the need to confess to my parents, but still I did not do what I knew was right.

Time went on. I prayed many times for the Lord to forgive me, but still I carried the guilt of that accident with me. As I mentioned previously, at the time of my NDE I was 31 years old. I had held on to my secret for almost 15 years. So sad! So much wasted time and energy!

During my life review, I was shown this scene very clearly and it was made known to me that this was one of the things I still needed to truly repent of and seek forgiveness for. At the age of 31, I still needed to talk to my parents and confess my wrongs. I learned with absolute surety that things do not just "go away." Repentance is necessary. We cannot do wrong and feel right, and we cannot enter the Kingdom of God until we have repented of everything that is wrong or not in keeping with the Lord's ways.

There are no short cuts. There is only one way back and that is through having faith in the Lord Jesus Christ, and in applying the Atonement in our lives. Even those very thoughts, words and deeds we do in the flesh that we think only we know about are written in the Book of Life. No one else on the planet may know we are guilty, but the Lord knows—and He cares.

It is through the power of the Atonement that we can be

forgiven for all things if we repent and come unto Him. That is the only way. He is the light, the life and truth. No matter what we have done, not matter how awful we think we are, there is always a way back if we are willing to do our part and repent of those things that need to be corrected. There is always hope.

CHAPTER EIGHT

———— ❧ ————

The Window of Heaven

After I was shown my life review, I was taken to another part of the room and was told to wait for a little while. John left me in the care of a few kind women, and he let me know he would be back shortly. A few men and women came and went out of the room. I could tell important things were being discussed, but it was unclear what they were working on or discussing.

I did my best to be patient, but I will admit that by this point, I was starting to get a little antsy. I had just had my life review, and I knew that I had several things I needed to work on. I had once again been shown more of what was going on at home and with my family. I was feeling ready to go back to my life.

John eventually came back into the room with a few men I hadn't seen before. One of the men asked me how I was doing and how I felt. I told him honestly. He then let me know it had been determined that I was to be shown more. He talked to me briefly about what he referred to as "The Window of Heaven."

He told me I would be shown many things, some of which were just for my knowledge and understanding. Other things could be shared with close friends and family, while some things could be shared publicly at some point in the future. He counseled me to use wisdom and discretion when sharing and discussing what I had been shown.

He cautioned me several times about the importance of being obedient and following the spirit of discernment. I was told that in no uncertain terms was I to share those things the Lord had entrusted in me, unless prompted to do so by the spirit. It was explained to me in great detail that it was extremely important that I listen to and follow this counsel and direction, and I was warned that if I did not do so, I would face very real consequences.

I was warned several times about the power of the adversary and those who would continue to try to distract me, deter me, and to interfere in God's plan for me. I was told that there would be many enlisted who would continue to try to discourage and destroy me, and to try to keep me from sharing my message when the time was right that the Lord had appointed for my story to be told.

I was given counsel and advice as to ways to avoid deception. I was promised added protection and guidance as I did my best to follow God's plan and to be obedient to His commandments. I was encouraged to put my trust and faith in the Lord and to rely on Him to the best of my ability.

I was shown that once I returned to my body I would be very ill for quite a long time. However, I was also promised that the day would come that I would be healed completely. I was shown that there would come a day, if I was true and faithful to the call the Lord had given me, that I would finally be able to open my mouth and tell my story. The Lord would prepare a way, when the time was right, for me to be able to serve Him and serve His children by sharing these experiences. I would be given the opportunity to testify of the things I knew to be true.

It was explained to me that although my body would be very sick when I returned, I would be protected and cared for by family and friends. There would be many challenging and sometimes dark days ahead, but I would not be alone on my journey. There would be ministering angels keeping watch over me and my loved ones, and as long as I did my best to put my faith and trust in the Lord, in due time He would provide answers along the way.

This was all explained to me prior to being shown "The Window of Heaven," and then reaffirmed afterward. I was given strict counsel about many things pertaining to what I had learned, and I was told that I would be held accountable for the stewardship given me. I was also promised that although there would be times of great despair and discouragement, and many times when I lacked clarity, the Lord would take care of things according to His plan.

I needed to remember to have faith and hope in the healing power of the Atonement of Jesus Christ and in His eternal Plan of Happiness for me and for all of Heavenly Father's children. I needed to listen to the counsel of my parents, my doctors, my husband, and most importantly the Lord. I needed to refer to and remember the promises in my Patriarchal Blessing, and to remember that all things are possible through Christ.

After being given this counsel and direction and agreeing to the terms set forth, I was shown a large window. I was told to look out or through the window and to listen, look and watch carefully at the things I would be shown.

The room was darkened as I began to look through the window. The scene started with a picture of what appeared to be random particles of energy floating around in space. It continued, and as the scenes progressed and changed, I began to notice that what I was seeing was what appeared to be an example of the beginning of the creation of the earth.

I saw that the earth had been created perfectly and that it is fulfilling its purpose. Everything about the earth, where it is located, its placement in the universe in relation to the sun, the moon, stars and other planets, and all of its beauty and the creations on it are part of God's plan. The entire earth and everything related to it was organized, created and is maintained by Jesus Christ. It was incredible to witness. I was only shown very brief glimpses of the phases of the creation and of the history of the world, but the overall message was very powerful.

I was shown once again that we shouted for joy when we heard the Lord's plan (see Job 38:7). We were excited for new experiences, and for the opportunity to come to earth to gain bodies and learn and progress. (See Genesis 1; 2:1-7; Abraham 3:22-23; and Moses 1:27-42.)

I saw that Adam and Eve were in fact among our Father's most noble and righteous children. It was made clear to me that Adam was called Michael the archangel (see Jude 1:9), in the premortal world. He was chosen by Heavenly Father to lead the righteous battle against Satan (see Revelation 12:7-9).

Adam and Eve were foreordained to become our first parents, and Adam was foreordained to be the first prophet of God on the earth. The Lord promised Adam that he would be at the head, and a multitude of nations would come from him and that he would be a prince over them forever. He was and is one of the most great and noble spirits who have ever lived.

It was made clear to me that the Fall was a necessary part of our Father's plan. It was actually a great blessing to each of us. Because of the Fall, we have been blessed to come to earth to gain physical bodies. We have been given the blessing and right to choose between good and evil. We have the opportunity to gain eternal life. Had it not been for Adam and Eve partaking of the fruit in the Garden of Eden, we would not have been given these privileges, and Adam and Eve would have remained in the Garden unable to fulfill all of God's commandments.

As is stated in the Pearl of Great Price, Eve said, "Were it not for our transgression we never should have had seed (children), and never should have known good and evil, and the joy of our redemption, and the eternal life which God giveth unto all the obedient" (Moses 5:11).

I was shown the importance of the Holy Ghost as a member of the Godhead (see 1 John 5:7). I saw that he is a "personage of Spirit." I was shown that although he can only be in one place at one time, His influence can be felt everywhere at the same time.

I was clearly shown that we have a very loving Heavenly Father, and that His son Jesus Christ, and the Holy Ghost, are called the Godhead. They are united as one in purpose, but they are three separate beings. Each has important assignments and roles they play in the Plan of Salvation. God the Father is our Heavenly Father and the ruler.

Jesus Christ is our older brother. He is our Savior and Redeemer. The Holy Ghost is the revealer and he testifies of all truth. He is the comforter. He warns us when we need to make "course corrections." He warns us when danger is near, and it is through the Holy Ghost that we can know the truth of all things. The mission of the Holy Ghost is to bear a witness of the Father and the Son and the truth of all things (See John 14:26; 15:26; 16:13; and Luke 12:12).

I was shown these things and many more through the Window of Heaven. I was shown some of the same things earlier, while in the library, and then I was shown them again, in addition to other things through the Window. The messages were and are so important, that at the end of my "viewing" I was again instructed to pay close attention and watch, look and listen. Once again, I was shown the same exact scenes and it was made very clear to me the importance of what I was being taught.

As is written by the Apostle Peter in the Bible, it was made very clear to me that "there is none other name under heaven given among men, whereby we must be saved" (Acts 4:12).

We cannot have faith in Jesus Christ without also having faith in our Heavenly Father. If we put our faith in them, then we will also have faith in the Holy Ghost, and he will teach us all truth and will comfort us.

I was taught that sacrifice means giving the Lord whatever He requires of our time, our talents, our earthly possessions, and our energies and abilities to further His work. As stated in Matthew 6:33, we have been commanded to "Seek ye first the kingdom of God, and his righteousness."

It was made known to me that our willingness to sacrifice is an indication of how we feel about the Lord and of our devotion to Him. Since the beginning, people have always been tested to see what their priorities will be and if they will put the things of God before all else in their lives.

The Apostle Paul wrote that "we should become living sacrifices, holy and acceptable unto God" (see Romans 12:1). According to the Lord, if we are to be living a life of sacrifice, then we must be willing to give everything we have for the building up of the Kingdom of God on the earth. We must labor to bring forth Zion. Only through sacrifice can we become worthy to live in the presence of God.

CHAPTER NINE

Earthly Cities of Light

As I continued to look into "The Window of Heaven," I witnessed many national events that have since taken place, as well as several that will still happen in the near future.

The nation was still experiencing economic trouble and there were small-scale natural disasters, but for the most part there wasn't anything to signal major problems ahead.

During this time, the leaders of the LDS Church scheduled a special meeting concerning preparedness that was broadcast. They also sent letters to stake presidents asking them to determine what supplies the Saints had and how much food storage they had. So meetings were held where local leaders passed out a list asking Church members to indicate the supplies they had available if needed. The list included axes, hammers, food storage, blankets, sanitary supplies, fabric, clothing, hoes, rakes, nails, horses, cows, and more.

These meetings enabled Church leaders to determine which families in their wards and stakes were temporally prepared, as well as determining those who were spiritually willing to share their possessions with others.

Then the invitation came from the prophet for Church members to gather at camps that had been prepared as places of refuge. Some of these were the previously established Girls Camps, while other locations were Church-owned properties that hadn't been fully developed yet.

This invitation wasn't a surprise at all to the Saints who had already been involved in the previous meetings on preparedness, but it came as a shock to the majority of the Church members. Most refused to even consider the idea of leaving their homes. Only a small percentage of the members went to the camps. The rest either did not have the faith, or they were not prepared.

Within hours of the prophet's invitation, everything was put into motion. White semi-trucks came, and they were loaded with supplies and food storage before traveling to the camps.

I noticed that the circumstances in the United States were not that bad. People were still working, going to school, and performing their normal daily activities. There was still power and electricity, and cars were still on the road.

The Gathering Begins

Despite these seemingly peaceful circumstances, the faithful Saints across the country heeded the prophet's invitation. The Saints throughout the Western states began gathering as they had been instructed, and I also saw hundreds of people driving from the Eastern states to the Kansas City area. They usually traveled in caravans, and some had two-way radios to communicate with other vehicles. There were some who came in campers and RVs, but I saw many vans and SUVs, along with several smaller cars.

These people had been organized very well, and they had been given strict counsel and guidelines for their trips. They had maps and directions, and I could see they were following specific, similar routes to get to their destinations.

They had been instructed to avoid certain cities and towns on their way. They could stop for gas, but nothing else. They seemed to be able to gas up at certain stops, and at other places they just went right on by, even though gasoline was needed for their vehicles. In a miraculous way, the gas in their tanks took them further than it normally would have.

There were some roads and highways that were very dangerous. These people did their best to avoid these areas, but on occasion, they were harassed and stopped by individuals and groups of marauders who had ill intent. There was a real sense of urgency that they arrive to their destinations in a timely manner.

Many of these people had left their homes without much prior notice. I saw them packing their vehicles quietly but quickly. The turnaround time for the initial group was only about twenty-four to forty-eight hours. There was a second group that left shortly after that, and then a third group that left later.

I am not sure how much time elapsed between when the first group left and the last group left, but it was only a few weeks at most. Some who were delayed—either by choice or other circumstances—still made it to the camps safely, but under much more dangerous and urgent circumstances. Many left too late and did not make it to their destination.

Just in Time

The last of these groups of people just barely made it to the designated camps as foreign troops hit the West Coast and were coming into California, which I will discuss later. It was as if these people were in a race for their lives. By this time, there were military helicopters, jets and airplanes flying over much of the United States, especially in the West. Police officers and military personnel began patrolling the streets and setting up checkpoints that limited travel throughout the country.

In response, I saw families hiking with packs into the mountains. Many of them hiked for great distances. Others did not have as far to go. Once they reached the camps, they immediately began to set up their tents in campsites that had been assigned to them. I saw people taking care of their children, making campfires, cooking meals, singing and dancing around the campfires, and talking one with another.

There was water nearby, but in most camps it did not go through the camp or alongside it. The campers had to fetch the water on a very regular basis. Most of the water had to be treated because it was not fit for drinking.

My Family Departs for the Camps

I then was shown my own family's journey from our homes to the places of refuge. We were assigned a particular camp in the Rocky Mountains. We traveled from the Kansas City area, in a southern direction to avoid Denver, which had become too dangerous for travelers. Then I saw us drive an alternate route through Texas, New Mexico, Arizona, and then into Utah. I saw us pass through the Moab area, then proceed north through Price Canyon in central Utah. When we entered Price Canyon, there were men there to help us through safely. We soon reached our place of refuge in the safety of the Rocky Mountains.

There was a strong feeling of urgency that accompanied these scenes. Thousands of others were doing the same thing. The majority of the Saints were attempting to reach campgrounds in Wyoming, Utah, Idaho, Montana, Colorado, and Washington, but I also saw camps in Florida, the Northeast, and other places. Some families temporarily camped in the Midwest on their way to more established camps.

I was shown scenes like this many times. One scene started out with an aerial view of the United States where I could see the various camps. There were other camps throughout the world, but most of what I was shown pertained to the United States. I was shown that the Lord will gather the righteous Saints to protect and spare them prior to the worst of the devastation and destruction. Then the cleansing will begin.

I also saw tent cities all over the country that were not organized by the LDS Church. These served as gathering places of safety for good people who were seeking refuge for various reasons.

Three Types of Camps

I was shown that there were distinct differences between tent cities, Places of Refuge, and Cities of Light. All three camps involved people living in tents, but "tent cities" was the general term for groups of people who gathered together when things got rough—due to famine, pestilence, martial law, economic hardship, drought, sickness, war, and so on.

These camps consisted of groups of non-LDS people, although there were some members of the Church there who had not heeded the prophet's call to go to Places of Refuge prepared for and organized by the Church.

The camps known as Places of Refuge were a step above the tent cities. They were organized by Church leadership, and for the most part the Saints were assigned to specific locations. These were mainly made up of active members of the LDS church, but in some cases there were non-members who were allowed to join the communities.

Cities of Light represented a whole different level. These were also organized by the Church and were places where the Saints were gathered with the intention to eventually live the Law of Consecration. In these Cities of Light, tent tabernacles and small courtyards were built for temple worship in the wilderness. As in the days of Moses, pillars of smoke were over the tabernacles by day, and pillars of fire hovered above them at night.

There were few Cities of Light compared to the total number of tent cities. Some of the camps that started off as Places of

Refuge eventually developed into Cities of Light.

I saw that many of those who endured these camps that were established by the Lord were then called back to establish New Jerusalem in Jackson County, Missouri. Not everyone, however, was called back to Jackson County. The Lord has an individual plan for each of His children, and Saints were serving in various places as they helped to usher in the Millennium.

Discord in the Camps

Some people who originally came to the Places of Refuge ended up leaving of their own accord. On occasion, there were some who were "escorted out" and forced to leave the camps because of disobedience. There were many reasons people left— not following the rules of the camp, stirring up trouble, false teachings, unwillingness to live the higher law, and so on.

Some just lost faith and gave up. Many decided it was not worth it and they would rather go back to Babylon, not realizing the great turmoil that was soon coming to the nation.

Children were born, people were healed from terrible sicknesses and disease, and in some cases people were raised from the dead. It was a true test of faith for all involved. There were some people who died in the camps, when others did not.

There were some who were asked to defend the faith, protect the camps, and in many cases to fight for freedom.

The first season of camping seemed to last a year or two. Then there was some type of reorganization where camps were moved or were combined into larger groups. This season lasted much longer—perhaps three years or more. It was during these experiences that the Saints learned to become a Zion people and they witnessed many miracles.

They also experienced tremendous trials and tribulations, but although life in the camps was very difficult, those gathered at these sites were far better off than those who had not. Many Saints who had passed to the other side were working as ministering angels. They played a key role in protecting the Saints, not only from real threat and danger from wicked men and women living on the earth, but also from demonic forces who were raging.

There were protective shields, if you will, placed around the camps, with varying levels or degrees of protection both from living priesthood holders who kept watch and guard, as well as from angels whose purpose it was to protect their children, grandchildren, great-grandchildren, parents, etc., from these evil forces. The Saints who had been gathered were protected physically and spiritually from the adversary as they worked together and obeyed the Lord's commandments.

Close-up View of a Tabernacle

As I looked down upon the United States, I saw the land become dark, except for spots of light in different parts of the country. This was both literally and figuratively.

I could see a few Places of Refuge in Colorado, and at least one in the state of Washington. I saw several camps in Idaho, Wyoming, and Montana. Most of the tent cities in Utah were in the northern part of the state, but there were a few near Moab and St. George. Some areas just had a mellow light surrounding them, while other areas were glowing with what looked like a small fire, which I felt were Cities of Light.

I then began to move toward the earth. The view narrowed in on one of the camps. As the scenery grew closer, I saw white tents, and several other tents of varying colors. Off to the side of the camp there was a huge white tent.

It looked similar to the pictures of the tabernacle the Jews had while wandering in the wilderness with Moses, although there was no altar in the courtyard area.

I could see a very bright light above it and it looked as though fire was coming out of the top of the tent — but it was hovering in place. The thought came to me that this was indeed a temporary temple. I saw people dressed in white clothing standing near the entrance of the tent, as if they were guarding it. There was a fence surrounding the perimeter, and two armed men were outside of the fence, guarding the area. I saw a man and a woman enter the tent after talking to a man dressed in white who was standing near the entrance. I heard the words "temple work" and the scene ended.

The view panned out again and I was looking at the United States from the sky again. I knew that the fire represented the presence of the Spirit of the Lord at these places. I am not sure how many there were, because the scene did not last long, and by the time I realized what I was looking at, I did not count them. It seemed like there were several, but there were more areas without fire than those with fire.

Another View of a Camp

Then I zoomed in on a different camp filled with dozens of tents. It seemed later in the year. I saw people dressed in warm fall clothing, preparing camp fires, fixing food, and cleaning around their campsites. Some were not adequately dressed for the chilly weather. They were wearing lighter clothing more fit for summer weather.

Off to the side of the camp there was a huge white tent again. The best way I can describe it was that it was a huge rectangle with a vaulted roof—like a very large wall tent. This one had a rock wall surrounding it, about three feet high. There were guards dressed in regular street clothes standing outside of the fenced area. This time I did not see anyone in the doorway of the temple, nor did I see anyone going inside. There was a pillar of smoke hovering in the air above the tent. It looked like a small gray cloud.

I later saw that winter had come. It was very cold and snowy. It was extremely difficult, especially for those who had not brought warm clothing with them. There were fires to help keep them warm, but it was very cold and windy. Supplies were limited and had to be carefully managed.

Some of the people were gathering at one of the campfires and singing hymns. Children were busy playing. I saw mothers caring for young children. I saw a garden area and someone was working in the garden, but I could not tell what they were doing. The feeling was peaceful and I sensed that the people gathered in this place were Saints. This was a very difficult experience for everyone, but there seemed to be a great deal of organization and order involved.

Assigned Roles

Camp members had been assigned roles and responsibilities, and everyone contributed and was expected to do their part. This was more than mere survival—this was spiritual preparedness for the return of the Savior.

I saw that the camps were organized into groups of families, with priesthood leadership and "captains" in charge of groups of 10, 50 and 100. Families camped together in their own campsite, but the camps were organized into groups so that several families were within one area.

Everyone had assignments and jobs in the camps, and each person played an important role, including children. I was shown that at least one of my jobs was to help with cooking and childcare. I saw myself tending a fire pit and checking food in a Dutch oven. There were children laughing and playing nearby.

The camps were orderly and clean. People had brought their own survival gear, but white tents were also distributed for some by the LDS Church. I saw many people reading scriptures, singing hymns and Primary songs, and praying. There were campfire discussions and group gatherings.

I saw some livestock, but not much. I mainly saw just horses and cows in most camps, but in a few I saw other livestock, as well as bee hives.

I saw four or five men on horseback and they were switching "shifts" with other priesthood men who were armed and guarding the surrounding mountain areas. Some men were keeping watch several miles away, and others were stationed around the perimeter of the camp, out of the sight of the children, but close enough that they could warn and protect the area.

I saw that my husband Jeff was one who was called upon to keep watch. I saw him sitting high up in a tree, overlooking the area, not far from camp. Later, I also saw him mounting a horse, with a rifle in his hand, leaving with two other men, to travel a greater distance from the camp and keep guard.

After being shown these people and some of their trials and tribulations, I quickly came to a much greater appreciation for them, and for my own life. It was made known to me that those who lived up to their foreordained missions in life, and particularly those who suffer and are martyred for Christ's sake, will receive eternal glory we cannot now perceive. All will be made right with the Lord.

CHAPTER TEN

Destructions, Famines, and Plagues

On three different occasions during this experience, I was shown some of the events of my life—past, present and future. I asked why it was so important to return to my body and my life on earth, and I was told several times that my earthly mission was not yet complete.

It was made very clear to me that we do not pass on from our mortal existence even a minute before it is our time to go. Some people may be given a choice to stay in the Spirit World, but in my case, it was made very clear to me that my time on earth was not over.

It was also made clear to me that in even the most tragic circumstances—in cases of accidents such as drowning, car accidents, and even cases of murder—the Lord is aware of all things. He takes even the most painful things we experience in this life and turns them for our good, if we allow Him to do so. He is always there to hold us, to comfort us and to guide us, but we have to do our part and seek Him. In the end, all will be made right. Justice will be paid.

The tender mercies of the Lord are also very real. In fact, often it is our trials and tribulations that build our character and help us become who we are meant to become. We pray for blessings, comfort and peace. We pray for healing and help to ease our suffering, and the Lord hears us. He answers our prayers in His way, and in just the right time and manner in which we need them to be answered. It may not always come how and when we want it, but answers do come. We can never lose hope. We must always seek to have faith in Him.

He loves us so much that He allows us to face opposition and go through the trials of life, so that we can learn what we need to learn to be able to return home to Him. He knows us individually, by name.

He cares. He listens. He hears our pleas for help. He knows exactly what we need. He allows us to experience the trials and tribulations in life because He knows that in the end it is all for our learning and good. We need to have faith in Him and in His eternal plan.

Having said that, I must say that sharing what I am about to share weighs very heavily on my heart. It is not easy knowing that something devastating is going to happen to you, or to someone you love. It is not easy trying to understand why the Lord has chosen to show me these things. For years I have prayed many times a day for clarity and understanding. I have asked "Why?" too many times to count.

I carried a very real weight for many years. The Lord forbade me to speak about my experiences, except for on a few rare occasions. I had been strictly counseled to be cautious about when, how, where and with whom I shared things. Some things I was told I could share with my husband, others with my children, and some with my extended family or very closest friends.

It was not until October 2013 that the Lord finally told me that not only could I open my mouth, but that the time was right for me to do so. I had a responsibility to testify of the things I had learned and know to be true.

The Lord has gently reminded me that His ways are not man's ways. He has counseled me many times to trust Him, to increase my faith, and to learn to listen more to His spirit. He has taught me that rather than asking "Why?" I am to ask "What am I to do with this knowledge?" and "How am I to serve?"

This is an important lesson I have had to learn, and I am still learning to trust in the Lord with all of my heart, might, mind and strength. I share my experiences in hopes that I might serve as a voice of warning and a voice of faith and hope. I do not share with the intent to invoke fear, although much of what you will yet read may invoke feelings of fear and anxiety.

I encourage you, as you read the remainder of this book, to seek the counsel of the Lord and ask for His direction and understanding regarding what I have shared and will yet share. I promise you that the Lord will tell you the truth of all things, through His spirit. Ask Him, and He will answer you.

Do not take my word for it. Go to the source of all truth, so that you can know for yourself what is true and what you need to do to prepare yourself and your family for the days ahead. Have faith in Him, and in His word. He fulfills all of His promises to His children.

The Earth is Suffering

One of the things I was shown through the "Window of Heaven" is that the earth is in great pain. Evil in and on the world has become so great that the earth literally feels it. This is in part why there have been and will continue to be increased natural disasters, plagues, and other devastations upon the earth now and prior to the Second Coming.

The earth is sick. The earth is tired. The earth is weighed down by the sins of mankind. The earth is in need of a cleansing. Because of this, there will continue to be upheaval. Droughts, famines, floods, storms, pestilence, earthquakes, and other destructive events will unfold. As the Saints seek to stand up for their beliefs, persecution will increase.

Internet sites and social media outlets will become a battleground of words and ideas as Christian morals and values are attacked from every side. Church members will stand for truth and gospel principles and help others see the folly of their ways, but there will be many members who will succumb to the enticing viewpoints and fall away from the Church.

I was shown that as time draws closer to the Second Coming of Jesus Christ, the weight of evil will continue to increase exponentially. Men's hearts will grow cold. Evil will abound in the hearts of many. The forces of evil have been and will continue to be unleashed as Satan and his minions intensify their fight.

At the same time, the armies of God have been and will continue to be strengthened, and the power of God on the earth will be greater than at any other time in history. The battle of souls will continue until the Great and Final battle.

Economic Distress

I was shown that the world economies failed soon after the mountain camps were established. I witnessed banners and signs declaring war, flood, famine, blood, fire, economic destruction, and other devastating circumstances. I was shown that banks were closed and money as we know it became completely worthless. Gold, silver and other precious metals were initially used, but that was short-lived and most people did not have the means or access to this.

We had to learn to barter and trade for our own survival. There was little to no manufacturing and commerce or industry as we now know it. Businesses shut down overnight—most without warning.

Civil Unrest

I saw rioting and mob violence start in the city of Chicago. Something bad happened to the Chicago airport, and other buildings in downtown Chicago. There were explosions, and fires broke out. Civil war began due to race rioting. Similar scenes played out in other cities around the world.

Marauding bands of people scattered in the streets, looking for opportunities to loot and steal. Gangs were prevalent. Mobs were in every major city in the U.S., and they went about murdering and plundering, trying to keep as many resources for themselves as they could.

The scenes I saw were horrific. They were violent, bloody, and disgusting. The hearts of many waxed cold. Men's hearts failed them for fear.

War Escalated Across the World

I was shown that war started in the Pacific. China continued to fight for control, and as tensions grew between China, Japan and other countries in that part of the world, the United States became involved as a dominant figure.

I also saw that Iran launched a missile from Libya, targeting Israel. Syria, Turkey, Saudi Arabia, and several other nations in that area of the world were at odds and the entire region was in complete chaos and turmoil.

Tensions between Russia and the United States continued to increase, and China and Russia joined forces in opposition to Washington.

The United Nations became divided, with some countries joining forces with the United States, and others joining the opposing side. The governments of the United Nations became increasingly wicked and fought for power and control.

Martial Law

I was shown that the United States government became so wicked that the citizens of the United States were subjected to martial law. The U.N. brought in "peacekeeping" troops, under the guise that the foreigners were there to help and provide food, clothing, jobs, and shelter. Their real intent was to divide up and conquer the United States, and to gain access and control of the food, water, and other resources that the American people and many other nations depended on for survival.

These foreign troops, along with members of the U.S. government who had aligned themselves with the global elites, had no mercy. They stopped at nothing to accomplish their designs. They spread lies to the people of all nations and did whatever they deemed necessary to divide and conquer. This included tearing families apart. They separated women and children from the men, and from each other, and went to great extremes to lie and manipulate situations in an effort to gain this control.

They used every fear tactic imaginable to accomplish their goals, including setting up concentration camps within the United States, similar to those used in Europe during the World War II era. They promised to take care of people, knowing individuals and families were desperate for food, water, safety and shelter. These were empty promises, however, and people soon discovered that they had been lied to once they were under the government's control.

Microchip Implants

In a similar manner, I was shown that many people were greatly deceived and willingly followed orders, feeling they had no other choice. Those in control of the people required a microchip to be implanted in the hands or foreheads of those who sought food, water, clothing, or shelter.

Some rebelled against those in force. This led to revolution within the United States, as people began to see the truth and recognize the need to fight for the Constitution and for their freedom. Utilities were limited, and in many cases, completely cut off.

Total power blackouts were commonplace. Food and water were contaminated due to natural disasters as well as man-made diseases. Conspiring men sought to control the population through the means of this food and water contamination, and other methods.

Gas prices, food prices, water prices, and other commodities increased exponentially, to the point that average Americans were unable to afford the luxuries they had become accustomed to. The standard of living went down so significantly that poverty abounded. Many starved.

Many schools closed. Government enticements continued to increase, with the promise of safety, security and prosperity. Conspiring men sought to control not only the hearts and minds of the children, but all of humanity. Their goal was to limit the freedoms of the people and one day ultimately control society, which was always Satan's plan of action.

Eventually, there was war in every nation. As time went on, the huge international world war turned into national wars, and then into smaller civil wars, as resources diminished and people rebelled against those who sought to control and dominate over them.

Bomb Threats

I saw that there were many bomb threats occurring at this time. Powerful bombs were actually set off in various cities. U.S. helicopters and military planes were seen flying all over the country, but especially above the western United States.

Signs in the Heavens

I was shown there were great signs in the heavens. Those who were faithful and were awaiting the coming of the Lord became aware and awakened, but there were many who did not pay attention or who were blinded and did not recognize the signs of the times. Many became afraid. The faith of every person was tested.

Earthquakes and Tsunamis

There were huge earthquakes and tsunamis all over the world. I saw several cities in the United States suffer great devastation. Los Angeles, San Francisco, Portland, Seattle, Salt Lake City, Boston, New York, Washington D.C., New Orleans, St. Louis, Houston, Chicago, and many other large cities became so dangerous that people fled for their lives on foot, carrying only what they could take with them at the moment.

I saw a huge earthquake hit Utah, devastating thousands and destroying most of Utah Valley and the Salt Lake Valley. Hundreds fled to the temples for refuge and safety. Water sprang up from the ground, causing severe flooding, mudslides and other destruction. Houses literally fell off the mountains, and others were sucked into the ground as the earth trembled and quaked.

Fires and tempests raged. There were massive lightning and thunder storms which struck homes, businesses, parks, and the surrounding areas. Many suffered because they were not willing to leave Utah's Wasatch Front—particularly their homes and possessions. In some cases they were required to leave friends and family behind, and many were not willing to do so.

Earthquakes were all over the world, some of which triggered volcanoes to erupt, particularly in the Western United States. Ash and smoke filled the air, causing darkness.

A string of devastating earthquakes occurred along the west

coast of North and South America, causing tidal waves to various parts of the world. Major cities were shaken to the ground, and some were overtaken by flood waters and tsunamis.

Huge Earthquake in Middle America

A short time later, another huge earthquake hit the United States. It began in the Gulf of Mexico, and continued up through St. Louis up the Mississippi River. It was such a huge earthquake that it was reported as a 9.0 to 9.5 on the Richter scale. It was so powerful that it twisted the Arch in St. Louis as if it were a soft pretzel.

Smaller, splinter quakes filled the region, affecting the entire Midwest clear up north to the Great Lakes. This huge earthquake was so powerful that it caused the great Mississippi River to flow backwards, causing a huge tsunami in the middle of the country. The effects of this earthquake were felt all over the United States and other parts of the world. A huge new lake and river system was formed that divided the country in half.

West Coast Destruction

Most of California was left in ruin by these earthquakes, and a great deal of the rest of the Western United States was torn apart and destroyed. The Space Needle in Seattle, Washington was destroyed.

San Francisco's Golden Gate Bridge was cut in half, falling into the ocean. Many of the great monuments of this country were completely destroyed, either through natural disasters or man-made causes.

The East Coast Suffers

Florida and the southeastern coast of the United States were also hit by earthquakes, although they didn't seem as devastating.

There was still great destruction in most areas, though, with power outages, water contamination, and food shortages. Some of the infrastructure was still left in place. Going further north up the East Coast, however, I saw huge devastation hit Boston, New York City, New Jersey, and Delaware.

I saw massive earthquakes and tornados storm through towns and cities, destroying everything in their paths. Homes and businesses were left in ruin. Flooding was rampant. Thunder and lightning storms were common, and they too left people homeless, desolate and without power and electricity.

The George Washington Bridge in New York City was destroyed. I saw the Statue of Liberty bombed, and the statue's arm holding the torch fell, with a huge wave covering it. There were more devastating earthquakes. It was as if the whole island shifted.

The Washington Monument and the Lincoln Memorial were left in ruin, along with other significant buildings, monuments, and memorials. The seas were rough and unsafe for travel. Huge waves completely overtook entire cities and communities, washing them away.

New Land Appears

I saw a land mass rise up in the middle of the Gulf of Mexico as a result of the giant earthquakes in that region. This new land was massive, extending from Florida all the way to Mexico. This land mass was separated from the other countries by water, with only a few access points to land.

Plagues and Biological Attacks

At this same time, I saw many plagues, drought, famine and pestilence, biochemical warfare, and natural pandemics. One of the plagues started with people getting purplish red spots on their hands or faces. People were panicking, trying to wash it off of themselves and their children.

Another plague was caused by a man-made biological weapon. I saw a man enter a large city in the eastern United States, go into the center of a busy downtown business area and dump the contents of a large vial-shaped container into the middle of the busy town square. It was about the size of a half-gallon of milk and the substance he dumped was a liquid that was somewhat transparent with a slight whitish hew to it. It was extremely dangerous and contagious.

The people who were around him in the city square were totally oblivious to what he had done. No one was even paying any attention to him. After the contents of the container were emptied, he quickly and discreetly left, blending into the crowd undetected.

This biological weapon was a disease that started with terrible white blisters of varying sizes that developed into pus-filled sores. Some of the blisters were quite large, and they appeared on the hands, faces, arms and necks of those who had contacted the disease. The disease caused confusion, dizziness, and complete disorientation for those infected. The victims often could not remember where they were, who they were, or where they lived. They essentially went crazy. They would come in and out of consciousness, unable to speak, walk or listen and understand coherently.

This plague started in the eastern states, but quickly swept across the country and spread quickly throughout North and South America. It was devastating. Interestingly, most of the foreign troops had been inoculated against the deadly pathogen, so very few of these foreigners suffered from this plague.

Posters were printed that people were required to put on the front door of their houses. The sign said "Plague" written across the middle with a large black circle around it and a diagonal line crossing through the words in side of what looked like a wreath. People were instructed on how to inform "the officials" that someone had died, and to report how many people were living in the residence.

The plague killed millions. I don't know how many—but I saw that it was so devastating that when someone contracted the illness, they were feared by all. Mothers and fathers cast their own children aside, in fear of getting the plague themselves.

The soldiers who handled the bodies of those who had died of the plague wore white contamination suits. Even these suits did not fully protect them from contamination.

I also witnessed another flu-like pandemic. It spread even more rapidly than the others. The results of contacting this virus were deadly. The scenes were horrific. Death often came suddenly for victims. It was so destructive and took the lives of so many that there was little time, ability or means for the living to give them proper burials.

I saw that bodies were literally stacked in the middle of parks and town squares, and entire cities were left abandoned. The stench of death was almost everywhere. People fled wherever they could as they tried to find safety, protection, food, and water.

Europe Erupts into Turmoil

The problems spread across the globe as these secret combinations began to execute their plans. I saw the Tower of Pisa in Italy blown up as part of an orchestrated plan that also destroyed other prominent buildings, including the Elizabeth Tower in London that houses Big Ben.

Soon after, I saw that the Pope was killed, and the Vatican was set on fire and destroyed. The wicked acts which have been perpetrated and will continue to be perpetrated by mankind are unthinkable. Yet they have happened and they will continue to happen on the earth until the day the Lord comes and Satan is bound for 1,000 years.

Trouble in Israel

Israel seemed to be under siege. I saw that the main Jewish synagogue in Jerusalem was totally blown up and destroyed, as well as the Dome of the Rock and the Wailing Wall.

During this time, an anti-Christ conspirator emerged on the world scene. I did not see his face, but he had dark brown hair. He was a handsome Caucasian who was a smooth talker and a sharp dresser. He became a "peacemaker" in the Middle East who was a deceiver—a true Gadianton robber. He aligned himself with the United Nations and the United States, and he made friends with many countries. He performed many "miracles," and even the very elect were deceived by his feats.

This same man knew and made friends with an Arab man who was also an anti-Christ. I saw the Arab man wearing all white clothing, including a white turban, shaking hands with the above mentioned Caucasian. They were both very wicked and conspiring men who sought power, control, and dominion over the people of the world.

Angels and Trumpets

I was shown scenes about angels and trumpets and the destroying angel passing by the righteous and those who had obeyed the Lord. Anciently, the sound of the trumpet was used to call the children of Israel to the door of the tabernacle.

The response of the Israelite people to the trumpet represented their public assembly and acknowledgement of Jehovah as their Master and King. Similar to ancient days, when the Savior once again returns to the earth, trumpets will sound, calling forth the righteous on the day of his coming.

Both the living and the dead will be called forth. Angels will sound the trumpets and those who are called forth will sing praises to the One True King. It will be a glorious day!

CHAPTER ELEVEN

Foreign Troops in America

In the midst of these natural upheavals, I saw war starting in the Pacific, as well as in the Middle East. The Iranians launched a missile from Libya that hit Israel. I could see that there were mushroom clouds throughout various parts of the United States, the Middle East, Europe and other areas.

Foreign troops who claimed they were initially there "to help," continued to assert their power and influence. Martial law ensued and the rights of the people were taken away. The troops used various means to gain the "cooperation" of the American people. They refused food and water to the citizens, and they held husbands, wives and children captive. In some cases they used execution. It was wicked.

I saw Russians parachuting into many spots along the coasts. Missiles were launched. The enemy proceeded, and I was shown that in many cases, people were protected by ministering angels who formed a protective barrier against much of the planned destruction. The foreign troops did successfully enter the country, but many of their missions were thwarted.

I saw additional foreign troops landing on both coasts of the United States, including Chinese troops, and some of what I believe were North Korean troops. Most of them were wearing a grayish green uniform, some with a hint of red on their hat and uniform. They landed first in Los Angeles, then soon after in San Francisco and on up the West Coast.

Large numbers of Russian troops entered the United States through the Alaskan coastline, and on the Eastern Coast of the United States. Russia came in through Alaska, New York and up and down the East Coast and northern West Coast. There were military helicopters overhead.

A huge world war began that eventually broke down into smaller civil wars within the various nations of the world. The war was over religious, political and social agendas. Wicked governments fought over land, oil, food, water, as well as for control of the land and the people.

The borders between Canada and the U.S. and Mexico and the U.S. were no longer viable. People from Mexico and other countries in Central and South America flooded the borders and invaded the United States, seeking to overthrow the little bit of infrastructure that still existed and to pillage and rampage.

Similar circumstances were occurring at the same time in Central and South America, and people fled to places of refuge there as well.

I was shown that prior to the Second Coming, the world outside of the camps was still in great uproar and chaos. War was everywhere. Governments sought to control, and the people protested and fought against those in power and against one another.

Safety in the Camps

It was made known to me that even after the earthquake in Utah the prophet and apostles were still organized and able to conduct business. They had prepared for these events and had planned accordingly.

It was made very clear to me however, that there was an

increased need for the Saints to listen to and obey the Lord. It became critical for each person to live in such a manner that they were in tune with the spirit and were thus led by the spirit in almost everything they needed to do.

While traveling to the camps and while in the camps, things were very orderly. They were organized and there was leadership within the camps. It was imperative that those who were in the camps lived in a manner that was conducive the spirit, so that they could hearing the promptings of the spirit and act upon those promptings.

There was a great need for each individual to be able to discern truth for themselves. This ability to discern directly impacted their personal and family safety and protection, speaking both temporally and spiritually. Increased faith and obedience led to increased guidance and protection from the adversary and others who sought to do harm—both the living and the dead.

Within the camps, people began to change for the better. They replaced the things of the world with the things of God. It required all of their faith. They had to have complete faith in Christ. It was a very difficult process, but it was far better than those trials others were facing outside of the tent cities.

I was shown that these camps lasted for quite some time. I am not exactly sure for how long, but it was for at least a year or more. I saw that the people endured at least one, if not several very tough winters. Within the camps there was a lot of conversation and speculation about when and where the Lost Ten Tribes would be gathered.

I was shown that men and women were called upon to fight for the freedom of the American people and for the Constitution of the United States of America. I was shown that some of my friends and family members volunteered to fight in this battle.

It was made very clear to me how absolutely critical it will be to have faith in Jesus Christ, and to have such trust in Him that we obey whatever He commands. Those who believed in the Constitution fought for our freedom and for our sovereignty. The battle was fierce, but ultimately the foreign troops left and we were left to rebuild the country.

Banners were flown, and opposition to the enemy was strong. I saw many banners with messages proclaiming freedom and government based on the constitution and liberty. Social, religious, economic, and political justices were proclaimed and the battle for these rights and freedoms was won, but not without much bloodshed and tears. Many lives were lost, but freedom prevailed and the enemy retreated.

Eventually, many of the Saints were called back to establish the City of Zion, also known as the New Jerusalem. In the Cities of Light, people lived the Law of Consecration. Over time, as the people's faith grew, more and more miracles were evident. When food shortages became a problem, the Lord provided manna in the wilderness, just as He had in the days of Moses. He also provided added protection through priesthood power of both the living and the dead. Angels surrounded the camps and resided within the camps.

There was a direct and constant influence of the Holy Ghost in these places of refuge. This was so obvious that it could not be denied. There was a lot of discussion about what people were feeling, seeing, and experiencing. Many wondered what was happening. The spirit taught and directed the people, and eventually, most came to an understanding that they were being prepared to become a Zion people.

Although the enemy outside of the camps could see the light coming from the camps, they did not know what it was. They did not realize it was the light of Christ—a literal light from God— rather than something being produced temporally by the people in the camps.

Enemy troops would try to encroach upon the boundaries

of the camps, but they were unable to pass. Thwarted by unseen forces, they were held back by the power of God. It left the enemy powerless, confused, and angered, and it helped to solidify the faith of the righteous. They began to understand more and more that light truly does dispel darkness, and that the power of light not only protects, it completely overpowers the dark.

Faith was increased, and with it came many more miracles. People began to look forward to each new day in the camps. Hearts and minds were opened, and the people rejoiced in gratitude. At some point in time, it became apparent to the people in the camps that they were being prepared for the return of our Savior. They realized that in the not-so-distant future, Jesus Christ would reign as the King of Kings and Lord of Lords, as had been prophesied.

I was shown the importance of showing love and kindness to others, and the importance of doing acts of service. It was made clear to me that it is essential that we show gratitude for all we are, all we have, all we will yet have—and that we are grateful even for our trials and tribulations.

In reality these difficulties are tender mercies of a very loving Father in Heaven who knows us so well and loves us so much that He steps back and gives us room to learn and grow, to suffer and sacrifice, and to make our own choices. He allows us to walk our own path.

He does this with the express purpose of being able to help us, guide us, teach us, and lead us back home to be with Him again, so that we may partake of all of the blessings He enjoys and that He so much wants for us to have for ourselves. He knows that these blessings are available to us only if we utilize the Atonement in our lives, and do our part to work and go through the necessary steps required here on earth for us to be able to progress as we need to.

It is as if from the beginning of the creation and onward, the Lord in His magnificence has created the greatest masterpiece. He is the greatest musical conductor of all time—the choreographer, the designer—knowing all and orchestrating things in such a manner that He knows exactly when to "bring in the strings." He knows when it is the perfect time to end one piece and move into the next one.

I was taught that even the most awful things that have happened, continue to happen, or will yet happen on this earth—God not only knows about them, but He planned ahead for them. He can turn even the vilest and most wicked actions of others and use them for our good. He does this not just in spite of the opposition, but often because of the opposition. He is able to perform miracles and create perfection.

I witnessed that after a thousand years of peace, Satan and his minions would once again be released and there would be a final battle. The adversary would rage with blood and horror, but ultimately the Lord's people won the battle. Satan and all those who had followed him were cast out forever, never again to hurt or torment man.

There will come a judgment day for all people. Every knee will bow and every soul will confess that Jesus is the Christ. I was shown that the Lord has provided the way and means for man to repent and to come unto Him.

I was shown that there really are places prepared for each of the Lord's creations, and that there are worlds without number.

We have a very loving Heavenly Father who has prepared a perfect Plan of Happiness for each and every one of His children. He is doing all in His power to help all of His children return to Him. In the end, God and His people will be victorious.

CHAPTER TWELVE

Adam-ondi-Ahman

During this experience, I was shown specific scenes concerning Adam-ondi-Ahman, which is an area located north of Jackson County in northwestern Missouri. When I was shown these things, the scene began with an aerial vision of the United States. Once again, like a camera with a zoom lens, I was given a panoramic view of the entire Adam-ondi-Ahman area, and then close up views of the sections of land there and in the surrounding areas.

There was a winding river surrounded by acreage. I could see that there were dozens of water wells throughout the area, supplying fresh water to the inhabitants.

It was here that Eve bore her son Cain. It was also here that other children were born to Adam and Eve, and their posterity began to work and till the ground. Adam and Eve were taught by God here, and it was here that the first death and murder happened when Cain killed Abel.

This was the place that the Atoning Sacrifice of Jesus Christ took on new and greater meaning and purpose for Adam and Eve and their family. I was shown that it is here that Adam built an altar and began to offer pure and righteous sacrifices to the Lord.

According to Doctrine and Covenants 116, in a revelation given to Joseph Smith in May of 1838, "Spring Hill is named by the Lord Adam-ondi-Ahman, because, said he, it is the place where Adam shall come to visit his people, or the Ancient of Days shall sit, as spoken of by Daniel the prophet."

Three additional verses of scripture also refer to Adam-ondi-Ahman:

"Three years previous to the death of Adam, he called Seth, Enos, Cainan, Mahalaleel, Jared, Enoch, and Methuselah, who were all high priests, with the residue of his posterity who were righteous, into the valley of Adam-ondi-Ahman, and there bestowed upon them his last blessing."

"And Adam stood up in the midst of the congregation; and, notwithstanding he was bowed down with age, being full of the Holy Ghost, predicted whatsoever should befall his posterity unto the latest generation."

"These things were all written in the book of Enoch, and are to be testified of in due time." (D&C 107: 53, 56, 57)

I was shown that before Christ descends openly and publicly in the clouds of glory, attended by all of the hosts of heaven, there will be other appearances. There are and will be secret and sacred appearances to selected members of His church.

Christ will come in private to his living prophet and apostles. Also present will be each of the prophets who have held the keys, powers, and authorities throughout the history of the earth, beginning with father Adam, to the present day.

At a later date, all of the faithful members of Christ's church who are then living, as well as those who have passed on to the Spirit World will be present as well. There will be a massive gathering of the Saints from all over the world and from all ages. It will be the largest gathering of the faithful in the history of mankind.

I saw thousands flocking to the area, dressed in the traditional clothing of their land and people. The people were organized into groups, by "tribes," each group representing one of the twelve tribes of Israel. They were camping in these organized groups, with leaders of each tribe, and "sub-groups" within the larger group. Similar to how things were organized in the camps, these large groups were organized by captains of 10, 50, and 100.

It was very organized and orderly, although at first arrival, there was a great deal of work and feelings of chaos amongst the people who were new and did not understand what to do or where to go. Those in charge knew very well what their purpose and mission was, and they did their best to instruct and lead the rest.

I saw three men in particular, wearing traditional clothing from foreign lands. They were being greeted by three Caucasian men wearing dark dress suits, white shirts, and ties. I could clearly see the faces of the foreigners, who had dark complexions. The faces of the three Caucasian men were not made known to me. They were standing directly across from the three foreigners, shaking their hands and welcoming them to the area.

All six men, and several others who were coming and going and gathering around these men, were located at the front door entrance of a tornado shelter area, and the door to the tornado shelter was open. My understanding was that these men were going to be given a tour of the premises and shown what was inside and underneath the shelter area.

These three men wearing tribal-type clothing were leaders of their groups and they had just arrived in the area. The three men greeting them, whose faces were veiled from my view, were from the United States, and they were in leadership positions.

It was made known to me that these three foreigners had come from far-away places, and they were a few of the members of the Lost Tribes. Earlier I had witnessed several scenes of the return and gathering of some of the members of the Lost Tribes. I saw that these people had come from all over the world, having been scattered centuries before. They came from Northern Europe, Iceland, Africa, Asia, the Middle East, and elsewhere. They had been led by God and had brought with them many of the sacred records of their history and people.

I saw that at least one of the three men in dark suits had dark brown hair and he seemed to be a somewhat older gentleman. The gentleman in the middle had a blond or very light brown hair color, and the man at the far end had medium brown hair. All three of these men were clean cut, with short hair combed to the side.

For those who are unfamiliar with Spring Hill, and Adam-ondi-Ahman, it is currently owned by the Church of Jesus Christ of Latter-day Saints. The church presently owns about 3,500 acres of land around Spring Hill. It is a beautifully kept area and has a very special spirit about it.

CHAPTER THIRTEEN

New Jerusalem and the Living Water

As time progressed, the people in the Cities of Light became more aware of what was going on around them and in the world. They started to realize more and more that the Second Coming of the Lord was getting much closer, and that they were being prepared to receive Him.

Although miracles happen to us every day in our lives now, we don't always realize or recognize them when they occur. Going forward into the future, the minds, eyes and ears of the faithful were opened and the righteous became much more spiritually awakened. People began to understand more and more the absolute importance of being faithful and obedient.

Hearts were softened and hearts were healed. Many were called to "open the hearts" of the children of God. As prophesied in scripture, the "hearts of the children will be turned to their fathers," even more so than they are today.

As the people in the Cities of Light increased in righteousness and faith, the protection they received from those who were on the other side of the veil increased tenfold. Miracles abounded and became even more evident in the lives of the people.

In one scene I was shown that an enemy approached the

boundaries of one of these tent cities. They had ill intent and sought to hurt and destroy those in the camps. Through the power of God, the enemy was held back. I could see that the men who sought to harm the people were angry, vicious, murderous men, who followed Satan.

They were extremely frustrated that they could not penetrate an invisible shield or barrier that had been placed around the outskirts of the camps to protect the Saints. Many of those who sought to harm the righteous were turned away, but in some cases the wicked were so evil and hard-hearted that they refused to back down and leave the area. As they attempted to force their way through, many of them were struck down by a force that was so powerful they died instantly. They did not even know what hit them.

Those who remained with them fled in fear and terror, all the more angry that their opposition had succeeded. They swore in their wrath that they would seek vengeance and that the people in the camps would pay dearly for their resistance. The men had no comprehension of the fact that it was the power of God that had struck their men down and prevented them from trespassing. They cursed God and man, vowing they would return with even greater force.

Some of these men left the group, but many returned. They brought more men and weapons with them. They were mad with rage. Once again as they tried to cross over into the protected areas, or as they tried to use weapons of force to penetrate the barrier, they were turned back. In some cases their weapons misfired, or would not fire at all. In other cases their bullets were deflected and the bullet would not penetrate, sometimes hitting the very man who had fired the weapon.

As these circumstances became more and more common amongst the people, the righteous grew in their strength and testimony. Their faith increased and they feared the enemy less and less. These and many other miraculous experiences solidified their faith. They learned that the pillars of light were not just their guide—they were there to protect them. They came to the understanding that the light increased in strength and power as they increased in faith. It was entirely based upon the faith and prayers of the righteous.

There were many who were healed from terrible illness and disease. The faith of the people was tested greatly, because some were healed miraculously, while others were not healed and in many cases died, even from seemingly small or insignificant causes. This caused some to question their faith and to waver in their testimonies, however for others, these experiences taught them the importance of relying completely on the Lord's hand in all things and trusting Him.

The difficult trials people experienced in the camps helped to lengthen their stride and learn to trust the Lord in all things, even when it came to those things that did not make sense to them. Living in the camps stripped the people of their pride and vanity. It stripped them of their need and desire to depend on things of an earthly matter. The process of sacrificing everything earthly eventually taught them to totally trust God and to depend on Him for all things. They gained confidence in the Lord as they increased their faith and obedience to His commandments.

I was shown that there was great singing and rejoicing in the camps, but also great sorrow and suffering. The people worked hard for their survival. They were tired—emotionally, spiritually and physically—but they rejoiced in the Lord. It required great sacrifice, but it was worth it.

Establishing New Jerusalem

I was shown that there would come a day when the Saints would be called back to establish New Jerusalem, and that Christ would reign on the earth as the One True King. I was shown that the earth would be cleansed and would receive its paradisiacal glory, and would eventually become the Celestial Kingdom.

Eventually, many of the righteous were called to establish New Jerusalem. The righteous who were called upon to usher in this great work of building the City of Zion were many of those who had suffered great persecutions, trials and tribulations. They were the true followers of Christ. Their mission was to establish New Jerusalem in what had previously been northwestern Missouri.

These people traveled there from the camps by foot. By the time they arrived at their destination, they were hungry, tired, and worn out. They had traveled great distances to get there and with much sacrifice. Most were in rags, having had very little to eat or drink along the way.

Once they arrived in the Great City, they were greeted by others who had traveled for the same purpose. Thousands of people became happily engaged in the great work of building Zion. Everyone had assignments given to them. Each person had a responsibility to work and do his or her part in establishing New Jerusalem.

I watched them build homes, businesses and other buildings. I witnessed them perform all kinds of manufacturing and machinery work. Lands were farmed and the city grew quite rapidly. Schools and churches were erected, and businesses boomed. The people were frugal, industrious, and hard-working.

Education was of utmost importance for the children as well as the adults. There were schools for people of all ages and all levels of learning. Higher knowledge was desired by all.

The Magnificent Temple in New Jerusalem

Buildings were constructed. Homes were built. A magnificent new temple was constructed in the center of the city. It was of a very unique design—a one of a kind work of art—like nothing I have ever witnessed on earth. It was incredible, made of the highest quality of materials. Once dedicated, it glistened in the sun and radiated light like I have never seen on earth.

Orson Pratt heard Joseph Smith describe the future New Jerusalem Temple. Elder Pratt said: "There will be 24 different compartments in the Temple that will be built in Jackson County. The names of these compartments were given to us 45 or 46 years ago; the names we still have, and when we build these 24 rooms, in a circular form and arched over the center, we shall give the names to all these different compartments just as the Lord specified through Joseph Smith. . . . Will there be any other buildings excepting those 24 rooms that are all joined together in a circular form and arched over the center—are there any other rooms that will be built—detached from the Temple? Yes. There will be tabernacles; there will be meeting houses for the assembling of the people on the Sabbath day." (Journal of Discourses, Vol. 24:24-25, October 26, 1879.)

I saw several views of the temple in the New Jerusalem. I witnessed the spectacular construction of this structure, and watched as those involved in the building process diligently listened to the spirit and followed divine guidance.

This temple was the most magnificent building I have ever seen on earth. There is no other building on the planet that compares to it. Its beauty and radiance defies all description, but I will do my best to try to explain how it looked.

As Orson Pratt said, the temple was actually made up of a complex of 24 square buildings, arranged in a circular pattern, covering dozens of acres. Each of these buildings alone was thousands of square feet in size. They looked to be about the size of the Provo Utah Temple. On the inside edge of each of these buildings there was a sparkling 30-foot-wide metal arch which joined in the center with the other 23 arches. This created a huge dome. Giant glass panels filled the spaces between the arches, and at the pinnacle of the dome was a tall, slender spire. This spire easily reached 1,500 feet or more. Each of the 24 "compartments" was magnificent in and of themselves, but the combined effect was truly astonishing.

I was amazed to see there were no support beams on the inside of the dome. Somehow, the arched design supported all of the weight. The 24 buildings were connected at ground level by glass-enclosed walkways. There were also elevated walkways. These elevated walkways connected the terraced flower gardens that grew on top of each of the buildings.

The meadow and flower gardens located at the top of the LDS Church's Conference Center in Salt Lake City somewhat remind me of what the New Jerusalem gardens looked like, although there is really nothing in comparison to the magnificence I witnessed. I had seen gardens like this during my journey in the Spirit World, but never before had I witnessed such beauty on earth. It was awe-inspiring. The light that came from the temple was extraordinary—its radiance and beauty seen and felt for miles around. It was truly exquisite. The design was flawless.

This temple and the temple grounds had been designed and built by the finest architects. Inspired by the Lord himself, there was absolute perfection in the work. It was a true masterpiece.

Both the living and the dead, including resurrected and translated beings, diligently worked on the creation and implementation of the design. Labors were performed by those specifically called of God. The New Jerusalem temple and the buildings and grounds surrounding it were the focal point of the City of Zion. It was so large and so radiant that even those outside of the actual city were able to see and feel its power. Its positive energy and influence drew thousands of people.

The temple served many purposes, one of which was to attract the righteous to this magnificent place. Many came from thousands of miles away, just to witness the temple and see the great masterpiece for themselves. Word spread quickly about the work that was being done in the New Jerusalem, and with that came more opportunities to spread the gospel. Thousands of people embraced the truth. Lives were changed. Hearts were opened. The people were enlightened, and knowledge increased.

The Living Water

In the center courtyard, not far from the temple, a tree was planted. From it sprang a variety of fruit not found on the earth. The tree was full of life and energy, as were the other plants, flowers and other vegetation that were planted. Beautiful fountains were constructed. A spring rose up nearby, and it was made known to me that the spring contained pure water—pure energy—and was "Living Water."

This Living Water watered the tree and other vegetation on the grounds of the temple and throughout the city. It sprang up in the cracks and crevices, spreading forth and nourishing and purifying the earth. It was used to water gardens, trees, plants and shrubbery.

The people soon discovered its purity and goodness, and drank it freely. It had a cleansing effect on their minds, bodies, and souls. It gave them pure energy, which they used in their effort to build the city. I learned that the cleansing power of the "Living Water" discussed in the scriptures is both literal and figurative.

Increased Health and Knowledge

The health and strength of the people grew, and with it their abilities to work and produce grew. They increased in wisdom and strength. Knowledge flowed abundantly and the powers of Heaven were opened. Legions of angels and many of those who had been resurrected came forth and aided in the construction of the city. Peace and prosperity abounded as the people anticipated the arrival of the Savior.

I could see that the atmosphere of the earth was changing. The cleansing process had begun and even though there was great devastation, the rivers, lakes and other bodies of water began to change. The earth slowly began to be purified. People talked about the changes they were seeing, and speculations were made.

Many discussed the "signs" they were seeing on the earth and in the heavens. Changes in the stars and constellations caused people to wonder, and many became afraid of the unknown. There was great confusion and panic from people all over the world, and some fear amongst even the followers of Christ.

Many came to an understanding that God's hand was at work and that these were "the Signs of the Second Coming," as foretold in scripture. The day the world had long awaited had finally come. Christ would soon reign upon the earth.

Unsealed Records

I saw unsealed records come forth in the latter days. This has been prophesied and I believed it would happen one day, but after seeing this, my testimony is solid. I am not exactly sure when, but I know it will happen prior to the Savior's return. Some were brought to the gathering at Adam-ondi-Ahman, and several records were brought by those who had come to build the City of Zion. I was shown that the records were made known to the people and that many of the mysteries of God were revealed at that time.

The Ten Tribes

Those from all of the tribes of Israel gathered to the New Jerusalem. Many members of the lost Ten Tribes came to the City of Zion. I saw some who came by boat, and others who came by foot. They came from various regions around the world. Although the gathering process had begun previously, the actual "Return of the Lost Tribes" as prophesied in the scriptures, came to fulfillment after the building of the New Jerusalem.

The Lost Tribes came forth from their hiding places and brought their scriptures with them, adding their records and testimonies to the scriptures we currently have. The mysteries of God were revealed and the people rejoiced. The Lord was in their midst and He personally greeted many of those who had gathered to this great city. Christ led His people and He managed the affairs of the city. The power of God was felt by all. Many were blessed with the abundant gifts of the spirit. Healings occurred. Miracles abounded. The righteous were reunited with their loved ones. Revelations were given and the people came to know their forefathers clear back to Father Adam and Mother Eve.

The Temple in Jerusalem Will be Rebuilt

I saw the time came when the temple in Jerusalem was rebuilt. I was shown that prior to the Savior returning to Old Jerusalem, the Jews began to rebuild a temple there. I was shown that they have been and are still currently continuing to gather supplies in anticipation of this event. Plans have been made and some of the construction has already been completed and is secured in a safe place.

At the appointed time, the Jewish people rebuilt the temple on the temple mount, in preparation for the Messiah. As prophesied in the Bible, they discovered that Jesus Christ is in fact the true Messiah, and many repented and came unto Christ.

Two Prophets are Killed in Jerusalem

I saw that there will be two prophets who will be maliciously murdered in the streets of Jerusalem in the last days, prior to the Second Coming. I could not see the faces of these two men, but I witnessed people rejoicing in the streets, happy that these men had died. I also witnessed the looks of shock and terror on the faces of those who witnessed the resurrections of these great prophets three days later. I witnessed the mixed reactions of the people as they came to the realization of what had happened. Some immediately repented, while others still hardened their hearts and continued in their wicked ways.

A Huge Fireball in the Sky

Once again I saw the earth from an aerial view in outer space. I saw a huge fireball approaching the planet. It was massive. It was brightly colored—orange, red and gold—like the color of fire. As this fireball hit the earth, fires erupted and spread all over the planet. I understood that what I was seeing was in part what had been testified of in scripture where the Lord has declared that the earth would one day be "cleansed with fire."

CHAPTER FOURTEEN

The Second Coming and the Millennium

I was shown that the earth would be cleansed and would receive its paradisiacal glory, and would eventually become the Celestial Kingdom. I was shown that those who had lived on the earth and were righteous would live on through the Millennium, where Christ would rule and Satan would be bound for a thousand years.

I was shown some of what it will be like when Christ comes again, and a brief overview of what it will be like in the Millennium. When Christ does come, it will be a magnificent scene. Every knee will bow in worship and praise of the mighty King. Tears of joy, humility, and gratitude will be shed. Men and angels will rejoice exceedingly. People will be in complete awe that the time has finally come for the Savior's return.

I was shown that it was a time of great joy and happiness. Word quickly spread of the news. Many did not at first believe He had finally come, but most quickly became aware and knew that He had arrived. Those who lived on the earth and were righteous lived on through the Millennium, where Christ reigned as the one True King.

In the Millennium, temple work was done for those who had

passed on but had never received the fullness of the gospel in mortality, or for those who had lived in prior dispensations and had not yet been given the blessing and opportunity to obtain these blessings.

I was shown that after a thousand years, Satan and his minions were released and had once again, in the final battle, raged with blood and horror. However, the Lord's people ultimately won the battle. Satan and all those who have followed him were cast out forever, never again to hurt or torment man.

I was shown once again that there was a judgment day for all people, and that every knee bowed and every soul confessed that Jesus is the Christ.

I was shown that the Lord had provided the way and means for man to repent and to come unto Him. I was shown that there really are places prepared for each of the Lord's creations, and that there are worlds without number.

I again was shown that we have a very loving Heavenly Father who has prepared a perfect Plan of Happiness for each and every one of His children, and that He is doing all in His power to help all of His children return to Him.

I was shown that in the end, God's purposes were fulfilled and all of His children received that which He has promised them.

My Return to Earth

The Window of Heaven closed. The time had come for my journey to end. I was overcome with emotion at the realization of what I had experienced. I was humbled. I was grateful. I was hopeful. I was encouraged. I missed my family tremendously, and I was ready to go back to my body.

I remained silent for quite a while. I contemplated what I had seen. My heart and my mind were full. I sat down in a chair, put my hands over my face and wept for a long time. Here and there John or other individuals would come in to check on me. They tenderly embraced me and expressed their love for me. They asked me how I was doing, and if there was anything they could do for me.

I thanked them several times for all they had done and for the experiences I had been given. They encouraged me to thank Heavenly Father, for He was the one who had given me the blessings and opportunity. I prayed and thanked the Lord for my many blessings and for the gifts I had been given. I thanked Him for the light and knowledge I had received. I asked Him to guide me and to protect me. I asked Him for strength and courage to be able to do what I needed to do. I asked Him to bless me that I would remember what I had learned and that I would recognize truth when it came. I asked Him to watch over me and help me to have the faith and courage to share my story when the right time came. I asked Him to help me live up to my foreordained mission and to live up to the commitments I had made.

Finally I was ready to go. In tears, I embraced some of my loved ones and said my good-byes. It was decided that John and a few of my distant female ancestors would accompany me back to the hospital room. We made preparations and soon I felt the light around me altered. I felt a kind of swooshing sensation all around me. I felt light and free as I felt myself traveling faster than I had ever known possible.

Within a matter of moments I was back in the hospital room. My motionless body was lying in the hospital bed. I felt a weight on me and around me. I felt a strange sensation that to this day I cannot fully describe.

The next thing I knew, my spirit and my body were reconnected. I felt a tingling sensation begin at the tips of my toes, the tips of my fingers, and the crown of my head. The sensation lasted for several minutes. It felt like pure energy traveling through me.

I slowly opened my eyes and looked around the room. I was

disoriented. I was weak. I no longer felt light and free. I felt the weight of my body and it felt extremely heavy. I sat up in bed. This took great effort. I was very light-headed and felt faint. I attempted to stand, and upon doing so, had to sit back down on the bed and rest.

Eventually I was able to stand successfully. I walked slowly toward the door of my hospital room. I could still feel the strange tingling sensation. I walked toward a large full-length mirror that was mounted on the wall next to the door. I stopped and looked at myself in the mirror, touching my face and arms, trying to make sense of what I was feeling.

At first I felt no pain, but after a few minutes, the tingling sensation stopped and little by little I began to feel an ache in my stomach, then my head and extremities. I felt thirsty. I felt hungry, but I had no appetite. I felt exhausted. My vision was blurry—in part because I did not have my contacts in or my glasses on—but my sight was worse than usual. It took several minutes for my vision to improve.

The door to my room was open and across the hall I could see the nurse's station, and I looked around in confusion. It took me a few minutes to remember where I was and why I was there. There were several nurses working in the area. A few were with patients in the hallway, one was talking on the phone, and another nurse was standing back behind the desk filing paperwork.

I walked out of my room to the front desk and upon my arrival I was greeted by a beautiful woman. I recognized her. She was one who had been assigned to accompany me. She smiled at me warmly and asked me if I was okay. I responded that I was feeling a little confused, but that I was fine.

I told her about the tingling sensation I had just felt, and she assured me that it was normal. I tried to tell her that I felt a bit strange, and I expressed my concern about what I felt was going on in my body. She seemed to know exactly what I was feeling, and was able to calm my fears and anxieties. I told her that I was very thirsty.

The others observed my behavior carefully. They were very concerned. When they heard me say that I was thirsty, they immediately took action. I was given a cup of water and they asked me if I was hungry. I told them I was, but that my stomach was upset and I didn't feel ready to eat anything. I said I was very tired and just needed to lie down.

I went back into my room and went straight to bed. I fell asleep again here and there, but tossed and turned. I kept dreaming about what I had been shown. My mind would not rest. The thoughts just kept coming and I kept replaying scenarios in my brain. Eventually I used the restroom and went back to sleep.

I am not sure how much time elapsed before the doctors and nurses decided to move me to another room. In this room I had a roommate. I don't remember very much about what happened right after I switched rooms, other than I know I slept a great deal. I was in a great deal of mental, emotional and physical pain. It felt like I hurt everywhere. I prayed for clarity and understanding, and I prayed for strength and healing.

Late in the evening I fell asleep again. It felt like I was in and out of consciousness. The veil was very thin. I continued to see, smell, feel and sense entities and spirits around me. It was intense.

Finally I cried out in agony to God, begging Him to help me. I pleaded with Him to protect me from the darkness I felt. I asked Him to give me strength and courage. I begged Him for relief.

In that moment, I felt a change in my surroundings again. I felt the familiar swooshing sensation I had felt before, only this time I found myself at the end of a very long, dark tunnel. All around me was darkness, with the exception of a tiny speck of light at the farthest end of the tunnel. I heard John's voice again, and I felt him beside me. I kept hearing him say, "Look at the light, just look at the light. Keep looking at the light. Don't look away, look at the light."

I followed his directions carefully, and within a matter of seconds, I had reached the light at the end of the tunnel. It had taken all of my strength to focus on the light and do as John had instructed, but I had made it safely. Upon reaching the light at the end of the tunnel, I could see John and a few others standing there waiting for me. They greeted me warmly and confirmed that I was all right. I was grateful to have escaped the darkness and was ready and willing to listen to them.

They asked me several questions pertaining to my previous experiences. They asked me if I remembered what had happened in the Spirit World. They asked me if I remembered and was still "on board" with what had been agreed upon. I told them that I did remember, and I asked for some additional guidance and direction. We discussed the plan once again, and I was given a short "review."

I am not sure how much time passed, and I do not remember how I came back the second time. I only remember waking up in my bed in the middle of the night with a strong need to use the restroom and a very hungry belly.

CHAPTER FIFTEEN

My Testimony of the Savior

The Lord's people have always had to sacrifice greatly, in several different ways. This has been the case since the beginning, and it will be the case until the final battle is won.

Some suffer hardship and ridicule for the gospel. Some have lost friends and family relationships because they have chosen to follow Christ. Many have lost jobs, and some have lost their lives. The Lord notices our sacrifices and He promises us great blessings for our sacrifice, obedience, and commitment to following His plan.

He has promised us that, "Every one that hath forsaken houses, or brethren, or sisters, or father, or mother, or wife, or children, or lands, for my name's sake, shall receive a hundredfold, and shall inherit everlasting life" (Matthew 19:29).

It is worth it. A place in our Heavenly Father's kingdom is worth anything that we may be called upon to sacrifice. As is taught us in the scriptures, it is through our sacrifice that we obtain a knowledge from the Lord that we are not just okay—we are acceptable to Him.

God has an important work for each of us to do here on the earth and in heaven. Work is an eternal principle. Jesus said, "My father worketh hithero, and I work" (John 5:17). Christ said, "I must work the works of him that sent me" (John 9:4).

So too, it is with each one of us. We each have an important purpose and mission to fulfill while on the earth. Our lives have meaning and significance. Things are not coincidental. They happen for a purpose, and that purpose is to bring to pass God's purposes—which is to bring to pass the salvation and eternal life of mankind.

I know this. I know that God is our Father, and that He loves us. He loves each and every one of us. He wants us to be happy. He wants us to find joy in this life and in the next. He wants us to be like Him and to have all that He has. He has provided a wonderful, perfect, eternal plan of happiness to help us fulfill this purpose.

We are not alone. We have a very loving Heavenly Father and our elder brother Jesus Christ, who watch over us and care for us. They have not abandoned us here on earth. They do not want us to fail—they want us to succeed. They have trust and faith in our abilities to choose righteously, and to continue to choose God's ways rather than man's ways.

There are ministering angels all around us—guiding us, protecting us, inspiring us, inviting us, helping us—and fulfilling their duties and responsibilities given to them now and in the preexistence. We in turn have a duty and responsibility to do our part in helping those who have passed on to become who they can become as well.

It is through our faith and obedience that we can be healed. We can change. We can improve. We can learn. We can trust. We can be perfected. Through the power of the Atonement, all things are possible.

I know this to be true. God is real. He is our loving Heavenly Father. Jesus Christ is the Savior of the world. He came to the earth to fulfill his foreordained mission as part of the Plan of Salvation that was designed and organized in the beginning. He will come again, and this time it will be in great glory, with concourses of angels and Saints singing praises to God on the Highest.

I have seen them. I have heard them. I testify of them. I know that any and all of God's children who desire to know these things for themselves can do so, if they put their faith and trust in God and seek after Him.

Ask Him for yourself. Do not doubt. Have faith and believe that you can know the truth of all things. He loves you, and He will answer you.

As we are counseled in the scriptures, seek not for the riches of man, but seek after Him, and He will bless you beyond measure. He is waiting for each of us to turn to Him. He stands waiting at the door, ready to answer, but it is up to us to knock. We have to do our part.

I am confident that in the end, no matter what our struggles, no matter what we are called upon to sacrifice and go through in this life, God will fulfill all of his promises.

As is stated in Matthew 25:21, I know that if we choose faith over fear, and are obedient to the Lord's commands, He will approve of our offering and will say, "Well done, thou good and faithful servant: thou has been faithful over a few things, I will make thee ruler over many things; enter thou into the joy of the lord."

I know this to be true. I testify of His love for you and for each of us. I testify of His great eternal Plan of Happiness. I testify that Jesus Christ is our Savior and Redeemer. I testify that He will one day return to the earth a second time, in power and great glory, to rule in majesty and love, and to take His proper place in the Kingdom of God on the earth.

I know that if we call upon the Lord and put our faith and trust in Him, we will be guided and protected from the fiery darts of the adversary. Although we may not understand why things happen the way they do, we can learn and know for ourselves what God would have us do, individually and collectively.

It is my testimony that if we are faithful and obedient, God will lead us by the way and will bring us safely home.

ABOUT THE AUTHOR

Julie has been married to her husband Jeff for nearly twenty years. They have three beautiful children, Ethan, Spencer, and Aubrianna. She is the second oldest of ten children. She was raised as a military dependent, and has lived in several different places: Utah, Texas, California, Washington state, New Jersey, Hawaii, Upstate New York, northern Virginia, Kansas, Arizona, and Heidelberg, Germany.

Julie received her Bachelor of Science degree from Brigham Young University in 1999, and her teaching certificate from the University of Saint Mary in 2010. She works as a certified Emotion Code Practitioner.

She loves camping and recreational activities with her family, and attending her children's athletic events and music concerts. She also enjoys spending time with extended family and friends.

She is an avid reader and loves learning about history, geography, science and a variety of other subjects. One of her favorite things in the whole world is to do family history work. She also enjoys meeting and talking to new people.

Julie has a passion for missionary work and a strong testimony of the importance of spreading the Good Word. She is very grateful for the tender mercies of the Lord, and has been a recipient of many. She is very grateful for the blessing and opportunity she has been given to share her story.

Julie can be reached at: **agreatertomorrow2014@gmail.com** or **www.healerslibrary.com** via the global practitioners map.